"I've always enjoyed Mike's accessible, conversational way of relaying what can be for some of us baffling territory. Independent Financial Planning: Your Ultimate Guide to Finding and Choosing the Right Financial Planner *is just one more fine example."*

-KATE FRATTI, award-winning columnist for the *Bucks County Courier Times* and *Doylestown Intelligencer*, part of Calkins Media

"You probably 'Do not know what you do not know' about the people you hire to manage your money and investments. Read this book before you invest your next dollar with a financial professional. Do not wait. You will sleep better at night and your future self will be grateful you did."

-CHUCK J. RYLANT, MBA, CFP®, author of *How to be Rich: The Couple's Guide to a Rich Life Without Worrying About Money*

"Even those of us who consider ourselves capable do-it-your-selfers when it comes to our finances can often benefit from the help of a knowledgeable and objective financial adviser. In this book, Mike Garry offers a clear, no-nonsense guide to choosing the right adviser and working with one most effectively."

-GREG DAUGHERTY, retirement columnist and former editor-in-chief of Reader's Digest *New Choices* magazine

"Among all the noise, greed, and confusion that surrounds the financial planning industry, Michael provides you with a fresh perspective and teaches you how to cut through the noise and find a financial advisor that is guaranteed to have your best interest in mind, not theirs. Not only will you learn how to find a financial advisor you can trust, but you'll learn about the ins and outs of the financial planning industry, and you'll come out feeling confident about your financial future."

-JAMES GARVIN, Marketing Consultant and author of *Bootstrapped*

INDEPENDENT FINANCIAL PLANNING

INDEPENDENT FINANCIAL PLANNING

Your Ultimate Guide to Finding and Choosing the Right Financial Planner

MIKE GARRY

First Edition, 2014

Manufactured in the United States of America

Library of Congress Control Number: 2013958285

ISBN-13: 978-0-9912587-0-3

Cover Design: Style-Matters.com
Cover Imagery: Shutterstock

For Rachel, Summer, Emma, and Amy

Acknowledgments

I'd like to thank my sister Debbie Pileggi and my #1 intern Alexandra "Allie" Bartsch, who both went over the manuscript and provided invaluable feedback. I'd also like to thank Robert Murray, Sarah McCarry, and the whole StyleMatters team. Sandy Diaz offered useful guidance and support throughout the writing process. Finally, my wife, Rachel, and my daughters, Summer, Emma, and Amy, were with me every step of the way as this book went from an idea to a reality.

Contents

INTRODUCTION

Why This Book?

Independent financial planning and investment advice is advice not tied to the sale of any of the advice provider's products. It's as simple as it sounds. Unfortunately, it's also rare. Choosing the right advisor can be like finding the proverbial needle in the haystack. You can't pass a newsstand, a website, or a cable channel without someone offering you financial advice—most of which is irrelevant, if not downright harmful. There are dozens of financial newspapers and magazines. There are even cable financial channels dispensing a constant stream of up-to-the-minute news and data. Portfolio managers tout their stock picks on the evening news. You're surrounded by information—but what are you supposed to do with it?

This book is designed to walk you through the process of choosing the right independent financial advisor and planning for your future.

In direct, no-nonsense terms, I'll tell you how to find the advisor who's right for you. I'll explain the basics of retirement planning. And I'll show you how to know if you're being hoodwinked by the very person who's supposed to be securing your future.

Why should you listen to me? I'm a Certified Financial Planner practitioner and a member of the National Association of Personal Financial Advisors and the Financial Planning Association with over 15 years of experience. Before forming my own company, Yardley Wealth Management, as well as my law firm, Yardley Estate Planning, LLC, I worked as an attorney at two successful Philadelphia law firms. I was also a financial advisor at Merrill Lynch & Co. and oversaw the operations of Global Investment Management. I am regularly featured in publications such as the *Wall Street Journal*, *Money* magazine, *Kiplinger's*, Businessweek. com, CNNMoney.com, and *Consumer Reports Money Advisor*, among others. I bring decades of experience to the table, and it's been my pleasure to work with hundreds of clients over the years to develop their individual financial plans and build security for their futures. To put it briefly, financial planning is what I do—and I love my job and working with my clients. You deserve an advisor whose greatest concern is your future, and I'll help you find that person.

Perhaps the biggest obstacle you'll face in your search for the right advisor is the fact that there's no single paradigm for dispensing advice that is best for all of those involved. I think a fee-only independent investment advisor who specializes in broad-based financial planning is the best model; but few people know about it, and it certainly has not caught on with the public yet. Financial planning as a distinct profession is still relatively new. (Actually, as much as it hurts me to say this, you could even make the argument that financial planning has not fully arrived yet as a true profession.) Accordingly, the industry is still in flux. While it used to be performed mainly by small financial planning firms, the last decade has seen many other types of firms entering the business.

Most of the larger financial service companies now claim to provide financial planning advice as part of their overall product mix. These larger financial service companies, where most consumers still go for financial products and advice, include full-service brokerage firms, online and discount brokerage firms, mutual fund companies, insurance companies, and banks. There are plenty of good, honest, hardworking professionals in these fields, but the way the industry is currently set up tends to work against the individual client's ability to achieve her financial goals.

You need honest, objective independent financial planning and investment advice that you can use in your own best interests. Unfortunately, none of these types of firm reward their workers for giving good advice. In most cases, their employees are not *allowed* to give clients independent advice. Their advice has to be tied to the sale of specific products, and they receive commissions for those sales.

The guy who says his advice is free when you buy his product isn't giving you a great deal. He's interested in selling the product because that's his job, and it's okay that that's his job. You might ultimately buy his product if it makes sense for you. What doesn't make sense is for you to hire him as your "financial planner" when he can't really give you any independent advice. He has a pretty big conflict of interest in the advice he gives you regarding the products he sells. It's just human nature.

An independent financial planner can work with you to determine the best products for your needs—and *then* a salesman can help you choose products that fit your financial planner's recommendation. What you need first and foremost is objective information tailored to your specific needs, and that's an independent advisor's job. While this two-step process might seem counterintuitive, I work every day with clients who have wasted thousands of dollars on unnecessary financial products. As with most things in life, a little time spent planning can save you a lot of grief in the long run.

So if independent financial planners aren't working on behalf of a corporation, how do they get paid? Financial planners use different billing structures; for example, some charge an hourly rate, some charge a yearly retainer, some charge a percentage of your investment assets, and some charge a fixed fee per service. What sets them apart is that they don't receive a commission. These independent financial planners have pioneered the art and science of financial planning. (Don't be fooled by the big institutions that call their sales reps financial planners or financial advisors and roll out their own canned financial plans!)

People often ask, "Isn't paying a percentage of your investment assets the same as paying a commission?" I disagree, as does the largest organization of fee-only financial planners, the National Association of Personal Financial Advisors (NAPFA). What's the key difference? The advice and the products recommended or purchased have no bearing on the fee, and the fee is paid by the client, not the maker of the product (as in the case of commission-based sales). When you buy a load mutual fund from an advisor, the mutual fund company pays the commission to the advisor. No matter what the independent fee-only advisor recommends, he will charge you the same fee based upon a percentage of the assets he manages for you.

The public is misinformed about most aspects of financial planning and investments, and as the fields continue to expand, the gulf most consumers need to cross to understand them grows even faster. This book is your bridge.

WHY DO I NEED AN INDEPENDENT FINANCIAL ADVISOR?

Let's face it—financial planning is confusing and overwhelming for most people. There's more information than you can possibly sort through, and too many voices telling you what to do with it. I have conversations on a regular basis with people who have no knowledge or experience with finance or investments who pursue all kinds of risky strategies: divorce lawyers trading options, doctors shorting stocks, and plumbers that day trade. They compound their problems by greatly underestimating the amount of risk they are taking. You go to an expert for everything else that's important in your life; you wouldn't try open-heart surgery at home! So why aren't you according your finances the same respect? Mismanaging your money can have drastic consequences. Don't shortchange your future.

The financial planning marketplace is very different than it was just a few years ago. In the past fifteen years the following common investment vehicles either came into being or reached mainstream acceptance:

- Roth IRAs
- exchange-traded funds
- 529 college savings plans
- Coverdell Education Savings Accounts (Education IRAs)
- Series I bonds

- Treasury Inflation-Indexed Securities (known more commonly as Treasury Inflation-Protected Securities, or TIPS)
- separately managed accounts (SMAs)
- hedge funds
- online trading.

All of these offerings have greatly increased the options available for consumers, and this freedom of choice is a great thing. Unfortunately, choosing wisely can be difficult, and sometimes having so many options makes it harder for people to figure out what to do.

As a financial planning practitioner, it's my job to keep myself and my clients properly informed. I stay abreast of ever-changing tax laws, research new products, and track down current and crucial information to help my clients make the best decisions possible.

HOW DO I FIND AN INDEPENDENT FINANCIAL ADVISOR?

The National Association of Personal Financial Advisors (NAPFA) (findanadvisor.napfa.org), the Financial Planning Association (FPA) (www.fpanet.org/PlannerSearch/PlannerSearch.aspx), and the Certified Financial Planner Board (CFP® Board) (http://www.cfp.net/utility/find-a-cfp-professional) have websites that can direct you to financial advisors in your area. I'd recommend looking for people working within a half hour or so of where you live. Study local advisors' websites and check out what services they provide. Are they the services you need? If possible, can you determine from their websites whether you fit the profile of the types of clients they serve? Call four or five potential advisors on the phone and ask whether they're taking on new clients—and if so, whether you fit their client specifications. Based on those calls, I'd select two or three to visit in person. I'll cover those in-person conversations in-depth in Chapter 4.

How do I know what information is reliable?

The truth? You probably never will—not on your own. And there's nothing wrong with that. Despite an abundance of information, most people are confused about financial planning and investments and where to go for advice. There have been tens of thousands of books written about these subjects. Numerous periodicals cover finance and money management, and a seemingly unlimited amount of information is easily available via other media, especially the Internet. It's no wonder most people are hopelessly lost when it comes to making financial decisions, or choosing someone to help them do it. We don't learn finance in grade school or high school, and most people don't take it in college. We typically learn about it from our families and the media, neither of which necessarily have any particular expertise. Many of the popular books tend to oversimplify things and make it seem as if anyone can read a 200-page book and then be completely prepared to handle all of their financial planning and investment needs.

Financial planning covers many subjects and each one is a distinct field of study. You need someone who can put it all together for you objectively, and that's where your independent financial planner comes in.

How does this book help me?

This book serves as an independent guide to financial advisors. I'll walk you through the process of financial planning, finding and working with planners and advisors, and the financial services environment. I'll help you figure out the best way to get help with your finances and show you the basic process and subjects that your financial planner should follow.

CHAPTER 1

What Is Financial Planning?

Financial planning is the process of properly managing your finances to achieve your goals. It is a broad area encompassing many facets of your life, because most life decisions involve money. Any money that you don't spend to support your lifestyle is available for saving and investing. How much you choose to spend or save, and what you do with your savings, will largely determine your lifestyle and wealth.

Professional athletes and Hollywood stars notwithstanding, most people have a finite amount of wealth and a limited ability to produce income. That limited wealth and income must support your lifestyle. You will not be able to afford to save enough for the future and buy everything you want in the present, so you will constantly face saving-versus-spending decisions. You'll also need to plan for the future.

An independent financial advisor can help you with all of these critical decisions.

Many financial planners belong to professional organizations that certify planners. The most notable one is the Certified Financial Planner Board, which is an independent professional regulatory organization that owns the CFP® and CERTIFIED FINANCIAL PLANNER™ trademarks. The CFP® Board, according to its website, is a non-profit organization acting in the public interest by fostering professional standards in personal financial planning through its setting and enforcement of the education, examination, experience, ethics, and other requirements for CFP® certification.

The mission of the CFP® Board is "to benefit the public by granting the CFP® certification and upholding it as the recognized standard of excellence for competent and ethical personal financial planning." In other words, you have to follow the CFP® Board's rules and standards to become and remain a CERTIFIED FINANCIAL PLANNER™ Certificant.

To become a CFP® Certificant and use the designation and the trademarks, a financial planner must apply to the Board and meet all of its requirements. These include extensive study and a ten-hour comprehensive test on the financial planning process and insurance, investment planning, income tax planning, retirement planning and employee benefits, and estate planning. There is also a work experience requirement, and the planner must agree to abide by the CFP® Board's Code of Ethics and Professional Responsibility. To remain a CFP® Certificant, the successful applicant must also complete continuing education equal to about 30 hours every other year.

The other prominent financial planning designations are the American College's Chartered Financial Consultant (ChFC), the American Institute of Certified Public Accountants' (AICPA) Personal Financial Specialist (PFS), and the CFA Institute's Chartered Financial Analyst (CFA). ChFCs usually work as agents or representatives of insurance companies; someone with the PFS designation is obviously a CPA. CFAs more often than not work as analysts or mutual or hedge fund managers but are becoming more involved in financial planning and independent investment advice.

I currently use the CFP® Board's six-step process with my clients:

1. Establishing and defining the client-planner relationship
2. Gathering client data including goals
3. Analyzing and evaluating the client's current financial status
4. Developing and presenting recommendations and/or alternatives
5. Implementing the recommendations
6. Monitoring the recommendations

The goal of the process is to help the client get a clear picture of her current situation, define her goals, and determine what she must do to achieve her goals. (I'll cover each of the six steps in more detail in Chapter 5: The Financial Planning Process.)

When you go to a financial planner for more comprehensive planning, you should make sure that she follows this general process. Obviously, if you just go to a planner to ask specific questions, this process will be abridged or modified.

BEHAVIORAL ECONOMICS AND SPENDING DECISIONS

Economists teach college freshman how people make spending choices by plotting graphs of the demand for guns and butter. At least in theory, individuals make rational choices as to how many guns and how much butter will make them happiest, given the total amount of money they have to spend.

For example, if guns are three dollars and a stick of butter is one dollar, and the consumer has ten dollars, which combination of guns and butter will make him happiest? Is it four sticks of butter and two guns? Or is it a single butter and three guns?

The choice is based on each consumer's perception of each good's marginal ability to make him happy. A rational consumer will want to maximize his happiness with his limited amount of money. Remember, it is the consumer's *perception* of what will make him happiest. Consumers are not always strictly rational!

Daniel Kahneman won the 2002 Nobel Prize in Economic Sciences for his work in behavioral economics, which looks into how our biases and emotions influence our decisions. Most decisions investors make are not based on a coolly rational, unbiased analysis of the subject matter. But while many choices investors make may seem to be irrational, the fact that they don't make sense to you or me doesn't mean they are necessarily unreasonable. People make choices based on their thoughts, circumstances, goals, and the information they have at the time they are making their decisions.

Because people have diverse values, they rank the importance of their particular goals differently than others might. An independent financial advisor will work with you and your own set of circumstances, not apply a boilerplate financial plan to your individual needs. What makes you happy is specific to you—and you should plan accordingly. There's no one-size-fits-all approach to your future.

RECOGNIZING TRADE-OFFS

Over your lifetime you will make thousands of decisions involving different trade-offs that will greatly impact your finances. Proper financial planning will allow you to make the most of your money and maximize your happiness by helping you to achieve the goals that are most important to you. There's no magic wand or pot of gold at the end of the rainbow—and the reality is, you will have to make some hard choices. Financial planning is all about balance. Ultimately, you will weigh your choices and their likely consequences to make your decisions and forge your own path. A financial planner can help you see consequences you might not have envisioned and can guide you through unforeseen obstacles as you look at your options.

Your goals also play a large role in your decision. If you are saving for a car, you will want to save money outside of your retirement plans to meet that goal, in addition to whatever money you are saving for retirement. Maybe you're putting kids or grandkids through college; maybe you've always wanted to take a cruise to Alaska. Determining how you will allocate your money to achieve different goals is a large part of financial planning.

I know talking about your goals and personal factors might sound a little too "touchy-feely," but how you feel about money, work, saving, and spending all goes into your decisions. The purpose of financial planning is to manage your money to achieve your goals, which are largely driven by your emotions and feelings. Again, here an independent advisor can help you decide which of those emotions are rational and which impulses might be pushing you toward unwise decisions.

CHAPTER 2

Investment Advisors and Financial Planners

Even if you decide not to use an investment advisor or financial planner, you'll still need to invest or buy financial products through firms that solicit financial planning and investment advisory services. In this chapter, I'll give you some background on how these firms work and how they compensate their employees, so you can be prepared to work with them on their terms.

1. FULL-SERVICE BROKERAGE FIRMS

What they are:

Full-service brokerage firms are institutions that provide stock and bond research, analysis, advice, and transactions. They create financial products, such as mutual funds, exchange-traded funds, and exchange-traded notes. They also do investment banking, which is helping companies and other institutions to raise money in the capital markets by offering their stock to the public (IPOs) and by underwriting bond offerings.

Pros:

Many of the big full-service brokerage firms have been household names longer than most of us have been around! Clients often appreciate the familiarity and security of working with a major investment firm. The firms' size—often tens of thousands of employees—creates an additional sense of security. And while recent scandals and crises in the financial world have taught us that even the biggest firms are not immune to crisis, clients still find comfort in knowing their assets are entrusted to a big name. Additionally, full-service firms offer multiple branches with similar quality of service, another feature that many clients appreciate.

Cons:

Thanks to my experience working at one of the largest national brokerage firms, I can clue you in to a secret: no matter how good your broker is, at his company, his chief role is as a salesman. He might rack up enough commissions to earn a fancy title (my old firm liked to promote brokers to "Vice Presidents"—we had thousands!), but he's still a salesman.

Why is this important? A firm's emphasis on salesmanship, instead of client satisfaction or solid financial planning skills, shows its priorities. These firms don't reward brokers for savvy investment advice or advanced training and education. They reward brokers for sales—and that means their brokers' focus is on the firm, not on you. The idea that a brokerage house financial advisor is a source of objective, conflict-free advice is, unfortunately, false.

When you go to an investment professional, you are really looking for *advice*, not a product. You are going there because you don't know what you should do or what you should buy—if anything. If you knew that you needed a certain mutual fund, you would have bought it. If you knew you wanted a specific life insurance product, you would have bought it. If you don't know what you need, you go to someone for advice.

When you go to someone looking for advice, you should not pay that person commissions. His interests are clearly conflicted: it's too easy for him to recommend the products that will be easiest for him to sell or that pay him the highest commissions. But it's your future we're talking about here—and you deserve better than advice that's biased because the provider of the advice is trying to make a buck. Does your lawyer try to sell you something for a commission when you go to her for advice?

You're much better off getting independent advice from someone who is not trying to sell you a product and who does not have those conflicts of interest. Why should you settle for being wary of your advisor's conflicted interests when you can avoid them altogether?

2. Discount/Online Brokers and Mutual Fund Companies

What they are:

I've lumped discount and online brokers and mutual fund companies into one category because their services are fairly similar. Most of these firms offer mutual funds and discounted commissions on trading stocks and bonds. You can usually speak to a representative of the company (not your own advisor per se, but a member of a call center), or you can do most everything yourself online. Historically, discount brokers did not provide investment advice or create investment products, but the market has changed enormously in the last decade, and many of the discount brokers are coming to resemble full-service firms in terms of the products and services they offer clients. However, the pay structure for their advisors tends to be less clear than with a full-service firm; not all advisors are paid by commission.

Pros:

For the most part, these are "do-it-yourself" operations. If you know what kinds of funds you'd like or are well-educated about trading stocks and bonds, these companies will serve your needs well. They offer a wide variety of products and a lot of independence. And if you're working with an independent financial advisor, they can be great resources.

I regularly advise investors to use low-cost index mutual funds and exchange-traded funds, and these firms are the best places to buy them. At our firm, we use two discount brokerage firms, Charles Schwab and TD Ameritrade, to place trades for our clients and custody their assets, and we use some low-cost mutual funds from Dimensional Fund Advisors (DFA) and Vanguard. We also have been a big buyer of exchange-traded funds from iShares® by BLACKROCK®. Your independent financial planner or advisor will most likely work with one of these firms.

Cons:

The drawback to these firms is that there's no one to provide you with investment advice. And while some of them are beginning to offer financial advising, as with full-service brokerage firms, their advice is hardly unbiased. Companies are far more likely to push you toward products offered by their own firms, even though they can sell you stocks or funds offered by other companies as well. While individual brokers might not make commissions, the *firm* does, and so its brokers will be inclined to prioritize the company's interests over yours.

3. BANKS

What they are:

In addition to the traditional business activities you would normally associate with banks, they will often offer a range of investment services similar to online and discount brokers—while they don't create products themselves, they can act as an intermediary from whom you can purchase various investment products. Bank representatives are able to offer investment advice and brokerage services. Many banks will review their money market accounts and contact customers with a significant level of assets in order to more aggressively pursue the sale of investment products.

Pros:

Banks may be good and useful in their traditional business lines, but when it comes to dispensing independent investment and financial planning advice, many are sorely lacking.

Cons:

A typical bank investment and financial planning offering will be a handful of load mutual funds and some annuities, sold by a salesman who might have been a teller last week. The former teller may be well-meaning, ethical, and bright, but he will also lack a knowledge base, objectivity, and independence. I don't recommend banks to my clients for any kind of independent financial planning or investment advice.

4. INDEPENDENT FINANCIAL ADVISORS

What they are:

Independent financial planners are not affiliated with any bank, brokerage, or insurance firm. Ideally, they will hold the CERTIFIED FINANCIAL PLANNER™ practitioner designation or one of the other major designations, such as Personal Financial Specialist (PFS). Their specialty is providing independent financial planning advice at reasonable fees. These are the best places to go for independent, conflict-free financial planning advice, because they do not try to sell you any commissioned products.

The vast majority of independent financial planning firms are small in size, with one or two owners and fewer than ten employees. A lot of financial planners even work in one-person shops.

Most independent financial planners are in the investment advisory business, registering with either the SEC or their state's securities regulators to provide investment advice. Remember that investment advice is just a part of what you would go to a financial advisor for, but it is how most of these firms are licensed and registered to do business. For most investment advisors, investment advisory fees make up the bulk of their revenues.

Pros:

Independent financial advisors offer you greater flexibility, services tailored to your needs, and objective advice on the best financial planning options for your individual situation.

With non-independent planners/advisors, everything clients do with them has to be through their employer's businesses. In contrast, with an independent investment advisor, you'll typically move your investments to a discount brokerage firm or a no-load mutual fund provider. You'd also sign a limited power of attorney (LPOA) giving your advisor the authority to make trades on your behalf, possibly vote proxies on your behalf, and withdraw his or her fee directly from your account. On that same account document, you would give the custodian the ability to do several things, including pay for any purchases you or your advisor make in the account with your funds and pay to the custodian any transaction or account fees. The independent advisor can then manage your stocks and bonds or mutual funds, depending on the type of agreement you set up with her.

The custodian is the brokerage firm, mutual fund company, or bank where your assets (such as stocks, bonds, or mutual funds) are actually held. The firm has "custody" of your assets. You'll have ongoing relationships with both your investment advisor and the custodian firm; you'll still get trade confirmations, monthly statements, 1099s, and anything else you would ordinarily receive from the brokerage firm and/or mutual fund companies, just as you did when you invested on your own. You'll pay that firm commissions to buy and sell stocks, bonds, and whatever else you might invest in. You'll also have an agreement with your investment advisor; she'll send you information and statements, depending on the terms of your agreement, and you'll pay her a separate fee for investment advice.

Cons:

- Asset-based fees

The advisor who charges you a fee based upon a percentage of your assets may want you to put more of your money into those assets that he manages, instead of using your money for other purposes. Remember, the more money he manages for you, the larger his fee.

For example, it might make sense for you to pay off your mortgage, or to pay down some other high-interest debt, instead of investing that money in the stock or bond markets. An advisor might tell you not to pay down your debt because he thinks your return from investing in the stock or bond markets will be better than your expected return from paying off your debt. That might be true, or it could be an entirely reasonable assumption based on the facts and circumstances. Or he might just tell you that because he wants to make more money from managing more of your assets. You cannot be sure which it is, so you need to be careful. Even he might not be entirely sure—that is the very nature of a conflict of interest.

Even if your advisor really believes that the better course of action for you is his managing more of your money instead of you paying down your debt, you can see where the problem arises. If you use $100,000 to pay down your mortgage, he gets nothing from that. If you add it to your investments that he manages for 1% per year, he gets an extra $1,000 annually.

- Investment-based conflicts of interest

Some Registered Investment Advisors (RIAs) don't provide any financial planning services. Some pretend to for its value as a marketing tool but aren't really all that interested in it or competent at it. Some RIAs provide comprehensive financial planning or wealth management services as a core part of their offerings to their clients. Those that do provide these more comprehensive services tend to have more successful relationships and more satisfied clients.

While I believe these more comprehensive services are a better business model for the advisor and offer a much more beneficial relationship for her clients, the arrangement can lead to a conflict of interest for these planners. Most of these advisors generate the majority of their revenues by providing investment advice, and most charge based on the amount of your money they manage for you. The conflict arises when the planner is telling you what you should do with your money. If she gets paid more for every dollar of yours that she manages, she may try to manage more of your money than she really should.

To reduce this conflict of interest with independent financial planners who also offer investment advice, you should make sure that you do all of your financial planning work first. Investment advice is just one part of financial planning, but since it is what everyone wants to talk about, its importance is sometimes overstated. Investments are just one part of your overall financial picture. That message bears repeating.

If you decide, after reviewing your financial plan, that you want your financial planner to serve as your investment advisor as well, make sure you stick to the dictates of the financial plan that was drawn up before the planner thought he might also get your investment business. Financial planning is not the same as investment management, and someone who does one of them well may not necessarily excel at the other. If you go to someone who provides both, judge his investment advice separately from his financial planning advice.

- A unique approach

Another issue to consider is that some independent planners/advisors are fiercely independent thinkers and the advice you get may be far from the mainstream. Obviously, that can be good or bad. I think in this industry it is a good thing to be far from the herd, but not everybody thinks that way.

If you want to follow the herd, steer clear of independent advisors. But I think most people would do themselves a favor by going to an independent and avoiding Wall Street and the herd mentality. Investing with the crowd in each year's "hot dot" is not a good strategy to pursue for your long-term financial health.

INVESTMENT PLAN #1: ROB AND AMY

Rob and Amy have a net income of $144,000 per year and have been saving for a long time. They have no debt other than a beach property in which they have a partial interest. Amy is 62, and Rob is 63. They have $50,000 in cash savings, and over the next two years plan to spend $30,000 on a car, $25,000 on home improvement, and $7,000 on travel. Their assets include a bank CD, a Schwab joint brokerage account, an annuity, some 401(k) plans from prior and current employers, a relatively large amount of pension income, and the beach property they are still paying off. Amy wants to retire immediately. Rob wants to wait.

My plan:

The most effective change Rob and Amy can make to maximize their current assets is to start managing their investments as a whole instead of in separate parts and according to a plan with an investment policy. (Nearly everyone who comes in to see me is in the same boat, so they shouldn't feel bad about that!)

When their CD matures in June, they can either renew it for another year (there or anywhere else that pays the best) or invest it. I'm torn on this because I know they are a little conservative, but between their cash savings and the CD, that's a lot of money not earning anything. Right now they have about $300,000 earning a weighted-average of 1% or less. While they need to have some money in savings that is safe, I think they can have substantially less, especially since their cash flow will remain so positive.

While Amy's gross income from her pension will be a lot less than what her salary was, since she is no longer saving for retirement, but retired, the difference in her net income will actually be fairly small. She won't be saving into her retirement plan or contributing to any other benefit, nor will she be paying state income tax, social security, Medicare, or unemployment taxes—and those things all add up.

Some other expenses relating to work might also go down, though I don't know if they will be more than offset by gas and gifts related to babysitting her grandchildren. They will know the cash flow change better after Amy has been retired for a little while. A rough estimate is that they will need around $700 per month to make up the shortfall before Rob stops working and before they start tapping into their pensions, retirement plans, or collecting Social Security.

That shortfall can be easily made up from some of the dividends and interest from the joint brokerage account. The best way to handle that is to have an extra $5,000 in their savings and money markets compared to the amount that ordinarily would make them feel safe ($35,000 in the regular one + $5,000 extra) as a cushion in case the distributions aren't quite enough. They can set up their Schwab account using its Moneylink program to automatically deposit $700 per month into their checking account. When they have a better idea of how their cash flow is shaping up, they can adjust the distribution if necessary.

Doing it this way means that they can allow Amy's Social Security benefit to grow and they won't have any extra taxes due on these distributions. Because the distributions come from dividends and interest, the couple is already paying the necessary taxes whether they are distributed or kept in the account. Also, I prefer doing it this way and having Rob max his 401(k) contribution to continue to get the tax savings. (They could make up the shortfall by Rob not saving as much in his 401(k), but then they would lose the value of those deductions. This way they keep the deductions and don't increase their taxes.)

If money starts to feel a little tight, they can figure out whether it is discretionary spending or inflation that has risen too quickly. They can always cut back on some discretionary spending if they need to, but if a loaf of bread is $12 or their heating bill triples, there aren't a whole lot of things they can do to completely negate inflation.

If inflation does get to them, they could certainly afford to tap into more of their taxable investments. Obviously, it would be a safer course of action to save them for some time down the road, if they can. While I prefer saving and prudence, there's no need for them to live like monks. If they need to take a little out here and there, it will have no impact on their long-term financial health.

As I wrote, they should tap into their taxable investment accounts first, because I would advocate keeping the tax-deferred assets in their accounts until they need to start withdrawing them at age 70 ½. If they need to take money from the taxable investments, they can always pick and choose what to sell to minimize their taxes. Also, the long-term capital gains tax rate is 15%, and their marginal income tax bracket (28%) is significantly higher. If they take any money from one of the IRA or 401(k) accounts, they will pay tax on it at their marginal income tax bracket as if it were ordinary income.

Finally, if they really run into cash flow trouble, Amy can always start taking Social Security, though I would advise that she wait as long as she can. It would be better to take Social Security than to take *material* assets from investment accounts.

What I have outlined is the order in which Amy and Rob would use the resources they have made available to themselves. Money should be taken from savings first and taxable investments second. If that isn't enough, then Amy should start Social Security, and their last resort would be to draw on their retirement accounts.

As for Social Security, I think the longer Rob waits to take it, the better off they'll both be. He'll probably take it when he retires, and hopefully that will still be a few years down the road.

Once he takes it, Amy can take her spousal benefit, which will be half of Rob's benefit. Then she can wait to take her benefit at 70, when she'll receive the maximum benefit. They'll have very good coverage in the event one or both of them lives a long time.

As Amy has a 98-year-old father, that would appear to be prudent!

I wouldn't pay off their shore property mortgage yet since they aren't sure what they are going to do with it, or what the time frame might be for selling their partial interest in it.

Investment planning:

Obviously, Rob's 401(k) must remain with his current employer. His fixed annuity IRA must remain where it is as well, or he'll be penalized for moving it. I think he's done the best he can, given these choices, but his 401(k) is currently heavy in cash and fixed income investments. I suggest he keep the current amounts but change future contributions so that more of them go into the other funds in which he's investing.

Having multiple accounts at multiple firms is not an easy situation to manage, and having multiple managers and/or funds within those firms means that Rob isn't delegating his investment management. Asset allocation and diversification is his to keep track of. Right now, he's doing a great job of keeping track of the totals and using a spreadsheet to track his accounts. Everyone should do this—but many of my clients don't, even if I ask them to!

The main problem is that Rob and Amy have no overarching investment plan to guide all of their different investments. Again, many people are in this boat—there's nothing to feel badly about.

Given the totality of Rob and Amy's circumstances, I would

ordinarily advise an investment policy of at least 60-65% stocks and at most 30-35% bonds in their investment portfolio because of their relatively high pension and Social Security income.

Those both act like fixed income, and they also have $200,000 invested in an annuity that works as a fixed income investment. Their school pension is $4,400, one former employer pension is $1,000, and another former employer pension is $400 per month. That totals $5,800 per month, or $69,600 per year. At current rates and their ages, that is equal to buying about a $1.1 million immediate annuity—so they can think of their portfolio as having that much more fixed income than it would without those pensions.

Rob and Amy are fairly risk-averse, so I suggest they adjust their other investments to a balanced 50% stocks, 45% bonds, and 5% cash. However, their overall situation is much more conservative than the 50/45/5 allocation I am proposing.

The problem with a portfolio being too conservative is that the fixed income and cash investments won't keep up with inflation. If you only invest in bonds and cash, your account balances go up a little, but you're actually poorer every year that there is inflation—and that is almost every year.

I recommend Rob and Amy consolidate their accounts. They can consolidate their investment accounts to: Rob's 401(k), their Schwab joint brokerage account, two IRAs for Rob, and one IRA for Amy. That's five accounts total instead of their current total of 11.

CHAPTER 3

How Much Will Independent Financial Advice Cost?

Most independent planners charge hourly or set fees for a financial plan, and those advisors who also manage money charge their fees based on a percentage of the assets that they manage (usually about 1–1.25% per year). That fee typically declines as a percentage as you increase the amount of money the planner manages for you. Many investment advisors include financial planning with their investment advisory fee.

The amount that advisors charge for financial planning and investment advice *really* varies. An industry commentator, Bob Veres, tried to get a sense of what advisors charged and what services they performed for their fees. In the July 2013 issue of *Financial Planning* magazine, he wrote that he found "a surprisingly wide spectrum of fee structures."

Independents made a big shift towards fees and away from commissions during the 1990s, and the broker-dealers have been moving in that direction as well. A small number of planners charge an hourly fee, and others charge an annual retainer that may be based on your investment assets, your total level of wealth, the expected amount of annual time your situation will command, or something else entirely. Many planners will use different fee structures for different clients, depending upon the clients' needs and their specific situations.

While retainer fees and annual fees are becoming more popular, they are still much less popular than commissions and fees based on assets under management. An annual retainer fee might be a better alternative for you than hourly billing, because you wouldn't be looking at your watch the whole time your planner was speaking to you. You also would be able to discuss your goals with someone who knows you, and if you had a simple question you could just pick up a phone and ask. An annual retainer might also work better than the assets under management (AUM) model, because it isn't based solely on the value of your investment assets. The retainer will be relevant to your individual situation and won't fluctuate every quarter because of market returns.

Of course, you may run into a problem determining just what that "relevant" annual retainer fee should be and whether it should be revised up or down each year based on how much contact you have with your planner or how much work you perceive that he is doing for you.

Neither advisors nor clients are flocking to hourly billing or annual fees—clients are not banging down the doors for this fee model, and ultimately it will be consumers who drive pricing. There is too much competition in the industry for client demands to go unheeded for very long.

Whether you decide on an asset- or a time-based fee, either is better than the commission-based paradigm they have replaced. The problem with commissions is that the broker's interests and the client's interests are not aligned. The broker gives the advice away for free but charges a commission to implement the advice. This of course leads to the broker having an incentive to recommend more expensive products or to trade more. At its most extreme, this leads to churning, or unnecessary buying and selling, to generate excess commissions.

CHAPTER 4

How Do I Choose?

Professional associations of financial planners include the Financial Planning Association (FPA), which promotes CFP® certification and was formed in January 2000 when the Institute of Certified Financial Planners (ICFP) merged with the International Association for Financial Planning (IAFP); the National Association of Personal Financial Advisors (NAPFA), a group of fee-only advisors (meaning they don't charge commissions); and the Society of Financial Services Professionals (SFSP), formerly the American Society of CLU and ChFC. I am a CFP® Certificant and a member of the FPA and NAPFA.

You don't need to find someone with one of these designations or affiliations to be assured of getting a good financial planner, but the designation provides a good starting point for your search, and most likely these professionals will follow the steps outlined in the CFP® financial planning process. Also, these professionals should hold themselves to the professional and ethical standards that certification or membership in their respective organizations requires.

There are many individuals in various professions who do some financial planning. Some of these people may call themselves financial planners but really only provide a small part of the overall process. You need to see what kind of process they follow to see if they are truly financial planners.

Some accountants and CPAs may provide financial planning advice in addition to their other services. If you are considering using a CPA for financial planning advice, look to see if she holds one of the other designations as well. Ask her if she is a CERTIFIED FINANCIAL PLANNER™ practitioner, Personal Financial Specialist (PFS), or a CFA Charter Holder and interview her as you would anyone else. Don't be fooled by the credentials that aren't really relevant to your needs. There are CPAs who really don't know much about financial planning but who see it as a source of revenue for their firm. Look for your CPA's commitment to learning the field and the process.

Insurance agents are licensed by the state they practice in to sell life, health, property and casualty, disability, and other types of insurance. Agents who can offer variable and universal life might also be registered to sell mutual funds. Be wary of insurance agents who can offer only insurance but insist that they are financial planners. I often see clients with some sort of permanent life insurance policy, such as whole life, who tell me they bought it to fund their retirement or to pay for their child's education. While there are many valid reasons to purchase whole life insurance, retirement and education planning are not among them. The policies do build up cash balances but much more slowly and more expensively than other investments that would have been more appropriate for attaining these goals.

The purpose of life insurance is to provide a death benefit. Sometimes you may want a permanent policy—to fund a trust, for example, or because your need for life insurance is not going to go away, and you need to buy a permanent policy at a time when you are easily insurable and can do so at favorable rates. Those are some good reasons to buy permanent life insurance. Don't buy life insurance to fill some *other* need.

As I previously mentioned, an investment advisor is someone who is registered with the SEC and/or their relevant state agencies to provide securities advice. Many independent advisors and planners are Registered Investment Advisors. If you hire a Registered Investment Advisor as a financial planner, make sure that she is concerned with your whole picture.

SECURITIES: WHAT TO LOOK FOR

When making recommendations or carrying out the purchase or sale of securities, many professionals in the securities industry are concerned about the performance of a particular stock or mutual fund but not about how it relates to your financial goals or your current situation. For instance, I used to get asked all the time by people who were not clients of mine, "What do you think of Johnson & Johnson, or United Technologies, or XYZ mutual fund?" I might know a good deal about the company or the investment, but I have no idea whether it would be a good idea for that specific person at that time without knowing a lot more about their situation, their goals, and their needs. You need to make sure that an investment is suitable for your needs. When you go to someone for financial planning advice, make sure you are getting financial planning advice, and not just investment advice. Investing is only one part of financial planning.

MONEY MANAGEMENT VS. FINANCIAL PLANNING

I wouldn't go to an investment advisor who considers himself a money manager. That implies that he is just concerned with your investment account, and not with your whole picture. He'll be intensely focused on the account and not long-term planning. There is nothing wrong with that, but it's not the same as financial planning. You have to know what you are getting into. An advisor who talks to you more about specific investments, algorithms, or accounts, and not about long-term planning or your future, is probably a money manager and not a financial planner. I sometimes see people who hold themselves out to the community as financial planners but act more like money managers with their clients' accounts. If you don't know what you're getting into, you will probably have mismatched expectations with the advisor, and the relationship will likely fail.

WHAT QUESTIONS SHOULD I ASK?

Imagine yourself as an HR recruiter seeking out top talent for your firm. You'd want to make sure to bring on the cream of the crop—and you'd want to make sure you knew everything you could about your prospective hires' qualifications. The same principle applies when you're looking for a financial advisor.

There's no foolproof resume or template for the right advisor for you. What matters is how well you click with your prospective advisor, how well she understands your individual situation, and how skilled she is in the areas you need her expertise. Oh, yeah—and whether you can afford her! In this section, I'll go through some questions you should be asking every potential candidate in order to ensure she's the perfect fit for your advising needs.

- "What qualifies you to offer financial planning advice, and do you hold any financial planning designations?"

She should be able to respond to this quickly and efficiently with details about her work experience, her educational background, any financial planning designations or certifications she has earned, and any professional organizations to which she belongs. If she can't tell you right away, I would worry that she has no confidence in herself. If she doesn't know why she is qualified, no one else will either.

It is not too difficult to find a planner with an educational background in finance or accounting, an MBA, JD, CPA, or other professional degree or designation, and the financial planning designations and affiliations I mentioned previously. Again, finding someone with this resumé does not end your inquiry. Rather, it provides you with a sense that the planner has some knowledge of the subject matter. There are many people who call themselves financial planners who have very little real-world knowledge. Ask her open-ended questions to explore her knowledge and experience, like "Where have you worked," "What types of clients have you worked with," and "Do you typically work with clients like me?"

There are so many planners with these educational and professional qualifications; you have to ask yourself if it is worth the risk to hire someone who hasn't gone through this intensive training. There are plenty of planners out there with this background. If you hire someone who doesn't have it, you had really better be sure about her.

- "What's your philosophy and approach to financial planning?"

If his eyes glaze over, that should be a strike against him. Financial planning is a great profession and many in the industry love their work. You will be happier hiring someone who is enthusiastic about answering that question, although sometimes you may have to reel him in!

- "What type of client do you typically work with?"

Will you be her wealthiest or least wealthy client? Neither position is particularly desirable, although every planner has a richest and a poorest client. If you are her least wealthy client, you may be neglected in favor of her richer, and by extension, more profitable clients. If you are her wealthiest client, she may not be equipped to handle your situation. There are different strategies and options available for those who are very wealthy.

- "What size is your firm?"

Another consideration is the size of her firm, both in terms of employees and clients, as well as assets under management for those who offer investment advice. There are no clear-cut answers here, either; it depends upon your comfort level.

Some people prefer to have a large-sized planning and/or advisory firm. There is some comfort in the fact that so many other people have made the decision to go with the same firm. With a large firm, you should be able to expect a well-developed process that your planner has gone through every time she takes on a new client.

You can also expect more depth. If your planner is out of the office temporarily, there is probably someone you can see in an emergency. Likewise, if she retires, or leaves suddenly, there are probably other planners similarly qualified and equipped to handle your situation.

The downside of a big firm is that you are less likely to have a very personal relationship with a specific advisor if the firm has five hundred or a thousand clients. As a client, you may gradually have less interaction with the person you originally signed on with as she develops her business.

With a small firm, it is more likely that the planner and her employees will know you and your situation very well. You can probably expect more support and individualized service. You are more likely to deal with the same planner and her team for the length of your relationship, and you may come to know her very well.

The downside of a small firm is that if something happens to your planner, her firm may go out of business, or you may need to look for a new planner. This, of course, might also apply if you work with a large firm—you might be unhappy with a new planner assigned to you and want to switch firms. But if potential for change is a big issue for you, you might want to work with a larger firm—even if you lose your original planner, you'll still have the familiarity of the firm you're used to working with.

To me, the amount of assets your planner's firm manages aren't an important issue. Some clients, however, like the comfort of knowing so many other investors have made the same decision they have. But remember, providing investment advice is not the same thing as providing financial planning services.

Because they are not the same business, many independent financial planners do not provide investment advice anyway. They'll make recommendations and may help you to carry some of them out, but they may not provide any investment advisory services for you or for anyone else. They may have no assets under management or only a very small amount that they manage for certain clients or people with whom they have personal relationships. It certainly has nothing to do with how good or bad they are at financial planning. You just won't use them if you want your financial planner to also provide investment advice for you.

- "Who will be implementing my financial plan?

You will need to clarify whether your planner will carry out her recommendations, whether she will refer others who will do so, or whether she will just give you recommendations and terminate the relationship. Since there are very few one-person firms, you need to ask which other people at her firm may be involved in your financial planning and what their duties are. If she is fee-only and you need to buy any financial products, she will be able to guide you, but not sell them to you.

- "Can I have it in writing?"

Ask the advisor to provide you with a written agreement that details the services that will be provided. *Actually read it, don't just recycle it!* Keep this document in your files for future reference.

How do I know a potential advisor is qualified?

I've covered the basics of certification, but that's not the only factor you'll want to weigh when making your decision. Next, I'll talk about key qualifications your financial advisor should possess.

- She has the necessary knowledge base.

For example, I have a B.S. degree in finance and an MBA with a concentration in finance. I'm a licensed attorney who took multiple finance and financial-planning electives in law school, and I'm a CERTIFIED FINANCIAL PLANNER™ practitioner. Those are the kinds of qualifications you'll want to look for when you're seeking out a financial planner.

- She can keep current with changes in the law.

The organizations that grant designations generally require some continuing education for their designees. If you are interviewing someone with a designation, make sure she is current. You can go to www.cfp-board.org and find out if a CERTIFIED FINANCIAL PLANNER™ practitioner is in good standing. Look for proven experience in financial topics and someone who keeps current by attending classes, courses, or seminars. Someone who teaches courses, classes, and seminars is even better.

- He has the right experience.

What kinds of companies has he been affiliated with in the past? How long has he been in his current situation? There's no magic number that will tell you how many years make an "experienced" planner, but you have to be comfortable with his answer. Remember, when you are looking for a financial planner, experience in financial planning, specifically experience with your type of situation, is much more important than experience in securities or the investment industry. There are many professionals in my former brokerage office who have been trading stocks since I was a little boy but who have little to no experience or familiarity with the financial planning process.

Financial planners tend to get clients who share some traits. Sometimes planners specialize in certain client situations or vocations, or income or asset levels. You're looking for someone who is experienced with your type of situation and has the right experience for your individual needs. If you have a middle-class income and lifestyle, a planner who mainly works with the affluent may not be a good fit for you. Likewise, if you are affluent, someone who specializes in credit counseling or debt reduction is probably not for you.

Ask your prospective planner what types of services he offers. His service focus will depend upon a number of things, including his credentials, licenses, areas of expertise, and most importantly, where he works. Independent financial planners usually offer investment advice in addition to their financial planning services, but some go even further. There are some financial planners who consider themselves "life planners" and who go well beyond the standard financial planning advice. Others counsel their clients on all sorts of things, such as buying computers or looking into nursing homes.

- You're comfortable with who benefits from her recommendations.

She should disclose relationships she has with other companies and with other individuals so you know whether she has a conflict of interest because of that existing relationship.

- Her career is free of disciplinary incidents.

Ask your prospective planner if she has ever been publicly disciplined for any unlawful or unethical actions in her professional career. You can verify her answer by checking with the authorities that regulate her business and the organizations to which she belongs. Multiple incidents will be hard for the planner to overcome, and I would have a difficult time hiring someone who regularly accrues complaints or discipline.

A lone incident should give you pause, but I would be willing to explore a relationship with her further *if* the planner acknowledges the incident when you first ask and can give a reasonable explanation. Remember, there are two sides to every story.

I have heard of and read about advisors who have had complaints lodged against them by former employers or ex-clients for reasons other than professional misconduct, and I've read that some brokerage firms have filed complaints against ex-employees who have left them to go to a rival brokerage firm. The complaints have more to do with revenge for taking clients than with anything the broker did in her professional life.

No matter what the incident was, if the planner lies to you about it, I would not hire her.

- You work well together.

Ultimately, once you've found a planner whose qualifications meet your needs, your relationship comes down to comfort. Would you be willing to spend significant time with her? How would you feel about her calling you? Sometimes you have to call your financial planner because things are not going well in your life. How would you feel about talking to this planner in a time of crisis—after losing your job, the loss of a partner or spouse, or finding out you are very sick? Would you trust that her finished work product would be of excellent quality and suit your needs? Would you be proud to tell your friends and loved ones who you are working with?

- You can afford his services.

You need to be clear right from the start how you will pay your planner for his services. As part of your agreement, the financial planner should clearly tell you in writing how you will pay him for the services he provides.

Once you know how he charges, find out how much he typically charges and how much he wants to charge you. While the amount you pay will depend upon your particular needs, the planner should be able to provide you with an estimate of the costs. If your expected fee varies from what he typically charges, find out why. Make sure the reason makes sense to you. If you feel the need, make him defend it.

Depending upon your financial situation, where you live, and the fee scale of the planner, expect to pay a thousand dollars to several thousand dollars or more for a fairly comprehensive plan, no matter how the fee is arranged. If you pay hourly fees, expect them to run from about $150 to $300 for most planners, and probably one-third to one-half of the planner's hourly fee for their assistants or para-planners. There is a great degree of disparity in pricing depending upon various factors.

All of these items should be spelled out in a written contract, consented to, and signed before any fees are paid or work is completed.

CHAPTER 5

The Financial Planning Process

In this chapter, I'll walk you through the six-step process of financial planning used by the CFP® Board. I've found it so effective at helping my clients clarify their financial planning goals that I use it in my own practice.

STEP 1: ESTABLISH YOUR RELATIONSHIP

The type of legal relationship you have with your financial planner depends largely on the type of firm in which he works. As I've said elsewhere, investment advisors have historically served a different function from financial planners, but these days there's tremendous overlap between the two titles—especially as savvy investment advisors realize they can give their services a marketing boost by billing themselves as financial planners. Additionally, there are a number of other types of investment and financial planning advisors. I'll briefly outline them here.

- Registered Investment Advisors

A Registered Investment Advisor is someone who is registered with the SEC or with her state's securities regulators to give investment advice. She charges fees for that advice, which is often related to the amount of money for which she is providing that advice. Generally, investment advisors register with the SEC if they provide this advice for more than $100,000,000 of clients' assets and with their state securities regulator if they provide advice on less than $100,000,000. The most common model for fees is Assets-Under-Management (AUM), and usually that fee starts around 1–1.25% and becomes marginally less expensive the more money a client has with the advisor. For example, if you had an investment advisor manage your money for you for 1% per year, and you had $100,000 with the advisor, the fee would be $1,000 per year. The firm would probably charge one-fourth of that in each calendar quarter.

By law, investment advisors are fiduciaries to their clients and have to put their clients' interests above their own, they owe their clients duties of loyalty and good faith, and they need to disclose all conflicts of interest.

- Brokers

Historically, registered representatives, or brokers, registered with what is now called the Financial Industry Regulatory Authority (FINRA) to broker stocks. They made commissions on the purchase and sale of securities (e.g., stocks, bonds, mutual funds, and annuities). So if you were to consult with a stockbroker, and he helped you to buy a stock, you would pay him a commission for the stock trade.

Not a lot of people out there these days advertise that they are brokers, and very few people in the retail financial industry work strictly on commissions today.

- Dually Registered Advisors

Nowadays, it's most common for brokers to be dually registered advisors who perform both advisory and brokerage functions. A dually registered advisor will offer a wide array of financial products in addition to financial planning services. She'll most likely be licensed as an insurance agent who can sell insurance and annuities and as a stockbroker; most dually registered advisors are also registered as Investment Advisor Representatives (IARs) so that they can handle fee-based accounts and offer comprehensive financial planning, or deliver a written financial plan. She will probably charge fees, commissions, or a mix of the two depending upon the products and services you use and the pricing strategy that her employer is using. This pricing will change in response to market conditions and her firm's marketing strategy. These firms have been moving towards more fee-based pricing, and away from commissions, although commissions still account for much of their revenues.

A pet peeve of mine is that these folks and many brokers say that they are *fee-based*, which confuses the public, and are not *fee-only*. Fee-based means that they manage money for asset-based fees (through specific arrangements their employers have with money managers) but can and will sell annuities and insurance for commissions. In essence, all they are saying is that they don't sell stocks for commissions anymore—and really, who does that today? If you aren't sure, the answer to that question is that hardly anyone makes a living buying and selling stocks on commission these days.

- Independent Firms

As I discussed earlier, an investment advisor is someone who provides investment advice and manages investments or accounts, and is paid by fee rather than by commission. A financial planner works through the financial planning process with clients and provides financial planning advice—again, for a fee rather than a commission. Small, independent firms are most likely to use the terms "planner" or "advisor." Most independent advisors use discount brokerage firms, such as Charles Schwab or TD Waterhouse, as custodians—meaning that these firms actually have custody of the clients' investment assets. Financial planning is not regulated per se, but the different functions performed by people who call themselves financial planners are regulated extensively. For example, the SEC and the separate states' securities departments and commissions regulate Registered Investment Advisors; the SEC and FINRA oversee brokerage firms and broker-dealers; and the states' insurance commissioners regulate the sale of insurance.

There are also hybrids of these basic firm types, and the ways in which these professionals work is pretty diverse. Many perform both financial planning and investment advisory functions for some or all of their clients. Because many of these people wear both hats, when I refer to one or the other, I am usually referring to the specific function that she is performing.

STEP 2: GATHER YOUR DATA

A key part of the financial planning process is gathering data about your needs, goals, financial situation, and risk tolerance. Your financial planner can't create a successful plan for you unless she has the details of your individual situation.

- Your financial situation

Your planner should ask for detailed information about your financial situation. She should ask for copies of your bank, brokerage, retirement account, and other financial statements; your tax returns; your insurance policies; your wills, trusts, and other estate planning documents; and any other pertinent documents. Your personal circumstances may require other documents, and your interview with your planner should uncover these. You will need to be forthcoming—your planner can't create a successful plan for you unless she has as accurate a picture of your financial situation as possible.

- Your goals

Some of us have never thought about our goals in concrete terms before, and some of us have each next step of our lives carefully mapped out. Regardless of which type of person you are, your planner will work with you to set clear, achievable, and tangible goals. If your clearest picture of your future is "retire young and rich," she'll steer you toward more specific (and possibly more realistic!) goals. While her job is to help you focus, it can be helpful to spend some time thinking about your goals in advance. Do you want to send your kids to college?

Travel the world? Retire at age 62 and live on 80% of your current salary? Save a specific amount to purchase a car or home? Whatever your individual goals may be, your planner can help you work toward them in a concrete way.

- Your risk tolerance

It is a basic principle of finance that the higher the expected return on an investment, the higher the risk associated with it. A United States Treasury Bill (T-Bill), which is a short-term debt instrument backed by the full faith and credit of the U.S. government (and its printing presses) is considered a risk-free investment. The government can and does *print* money to pay you back, and it always has, so it is considered to be the only risk-free investment.

Risk-free in this instance means there is no risk in getting back the money you have invested, plus the interest or return on your investment that you were guaranteed by the borrower (the borrower in this instance being the U.S. Treasury). Of course, if the government decides to print too much money, it might lead to inflation, which will erode the value of your investment. So even this risk-free investment has *some* risk—no wonder people have a hard time with financial planning and investments!

Every other investment has a higher element of risk.

The graph on the next page shows the largest, most commonly referred to investment assets. Ideally, you should own some of these different types of investments in a way that provides the return necessary to achieve your goals while minimizing your risk. Any extra risk is unnecessary and actually counterproductive. You might have less of a chance of meeting your goals if you take on too much risk.

FIGURE 5.1: *Risk/Reward Spectrum*

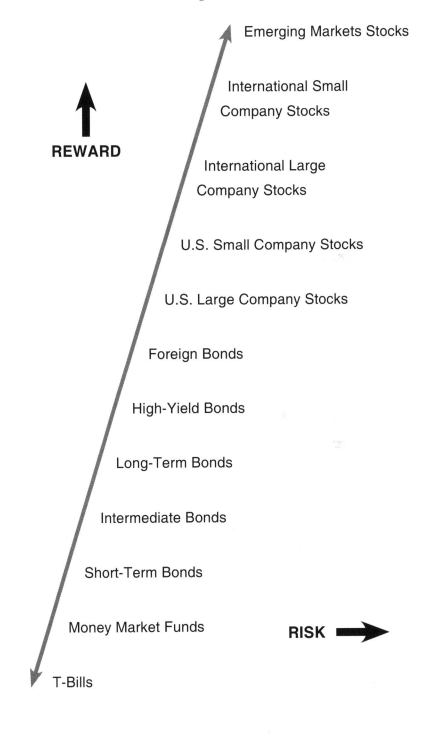

STEP 3: EVALUATE YOUR FINANCIAL STATUS

Your planner has all your financial information; now, she'll analyze the data you've given her and determine the next steps toward your goals.

There's no hard and fast rule for what your plan will look like: again, this is why it's so important for you to find a planner with whom you work well and who understands the details of your individual situation. Your planner can help you as much—or as little—as you'd like; she can work with you to lay out a detailed, step-by-step plan or to set general guidelines for how to manage your assets.

She should be upfront about any areas in which you need expert help—for example, she might not know the inner workings of property and casualty insurance. That's perfectly fine, but you'll want to be sure she's able to find the answer for you or direct you toward the help you need. Never assume that the information you're looking for is too technical or specific—while there's no way for her to know the answer to any question you could possibly ask her, it's her job to work with you to find the information you need to make the best decisions possible.

STEP 4: ASSESS YOUR PLANNER'S RECOMMENDATIONS

At this point, the fourth step in the planning process, your planner will present you with recommendations and an appropriate course of action. His recommendations should directly address your goals and incorporate the information you've given him about your financial situation. He should go over the recommendations with you, evaluate any concerns you may have, and revise his recommendations where appropriate.

Most planners will give you a written set of recommendations—some might even present you with a binder or a bound book. Again, there's no uniform procedure—what matters is that you clearly understand the information you've been given and that your planner is able and willing to address any questions you might have. You should feel comfortable asking questions, and your planner should answer them thoroughly. You'll also want to determine who will be responsible for tracking your progress toward your goals once the recommendations are put into action.

STEP 5: IMPLEMENT YOUR RECOMMENDATIONS

Now, it's time to set your financial plan in motion.

The extent to which your planner will carry out her recommendations herself depends on the type of relationship you set up in Step 1. If she works at a large bank, brokerage firm, or insurance company, she'll likely implement the majority of the plan herself; if she works as an independent planner, you may be responsible for more of the implementation.

If you've chosen to work with a large brokerage firm, you'll want to keep a sharp eye out to ensure your planner isn't trying to sell you unneeded products as part of her plan. Again, stay aware of any conflicts of interest—your plan shouldn't be dependent on specific products or services she benefits from selling you.

FLAWED RETIREE WITHDRAWAL PLAN

When figuring out how much they can safely withdraw from a retirement portfolio, a lot of people use a straight-line model. In a straight-line model, the standard software assumes that every year you earn an average return and remove a fixed dollar amount, adjusted for inflation. This is a big mistake.

Why? Because there's no guarantee that things will go so smoothly. If the past few years have demonstrated anything, it is that you can't plan for a future of stable returns. For example, assuming that your portfolio is half in stocks and half in bonds, the software may assume that you will earn 6% per year, every year, and that any withdrawal amount less than that will work forever, without your ever running out of money.

This type of software, and this scenario, will show you earning money *ad infinitum*. If you have $500,000, the software will tell you that any withdrawal sum under $30,000 (6% of $500,000) will work out fine and that the excess amount will be added back to your principal over and over again. That's a nice theory—but it doesn't work often enough to be reliable. If you retire at the beginning of a bear market, a time when stocks generally go down 20% from their previous highs, you'll run out of money much faster than the straight-line method predicts.

Let's go through one more example to show what can happen. Let's say this year things are going well. You're starting with

$500,000, expecting and getting a 6% return, and using a 5% withdrawal rate. So far, so good. At the end of this first year, you expect to have $505,000, or $5,000 more than you started with—even factoring in a large withdrawal of $25,000, or 5% of your portfolio.

However, what if bonds provide their expected 4% return, but stocks go down 20%, and you still take out $25,000? Your portfolio suffers an 8% loss, and you've compounded the decline even further by taking out 5% of the starting value. You'll end the year at $435,000.

This is a recipe for running out of money fast. After just one bad year, you have about 13.8% less than the $505,000 you thought you would. Even if your second year of returns are flat, by the end of *that* year you'll have just $410,000 left in your account.

What if one bad year turns into more bad years, like it did in the aftermath of the financial crisis and recession? These years were rough primarily on stocks—most bonds did well during the recent equities bear market. Proper asset allocation can do a lot to cushion that type of blow. But if, like many people, you didn't have enough money in bonds during the bear market years—well, you don't need me to tell you that you were in trouble. And what happens when both stocks *and* bonds do poorly for a few years? It's happened before, and it will happen again.

In short: the straight-line method is clearly not the way to go. It's incredibly important to allocate your resources wisely—and it's just as important to adjust your withdrawal rate.

Step 6: Monitor Your Progress

You've implemented your plan: now it's time to track your progress toward your goals. Whether you or your planner is responsible for charting your path depends on the relationship you've set up—and that's something you'll want to establish before your plan is implemented. If he's the one who's keeping an eye on things, he should report to you periodically to review your situation and adjust your plan as needed.

How often you and your planner are in contact depends on the terms you set at the start of the relationship, but you can always adjust your contact level if the frequency seems off once your plan's in place. In my own practice, I call or meet with different clients with varying degrees of frequency depending on their needs and situation. Some clients I see quarterly; others, less than once a year. It's not uncommon for your planner to meet with you quite often at the beginning of your relationship and then decrease that frequency once your plan is implemented and has proven effective.

It might sound counterintuitive, but I'd actually advise against meeting too often. Once your plan is implemented, you'll only need to adjust it when there are major changes to your life circumstances (for example, a raise or an inheritance) or to the financial planning landscape. You'll want to make sure that you and your planner are staying on track with your goals, but you don't need to focus on the minor ups and downs of the market or the small surprises of daily life. This holds true for investment advice, too—there's no reason to constantly buy and sell just because of minor fluctuations in the market. Remember what they said about the tortoise—slow and steady wins the race.

Last but not least, your planner should let you know ahead of time how much—and if—it will cost you to call her or meet with her in person. And remember, if you're uncomfortable calling your planner, there's something wrong with your relationship. Open communication is critical for a successful partnership.

INVESTMENT PLAN: RICHARD

Richard is a 50-year-old single dad in good financial shape. His young daughter, Emma, will still be in high school in ten years when he hopes to retire. He is a modest spender, his income greatly exceeds his spending, and he works for a company that still provides a pension. He is interested in financial planning and investing, and he thinks he might be moving in the next few years.

My plan:

Richard lives well within his means, so I'm not concerned about his cash flow. He spends about four to five thousand dollars a month, half of which is his mortgage. I like to see people pay off their mortgages before retiring, and Richard's won't be paid off until he's 80 if he keeps making the regularly scheduled payments. However, since Richard plans to move, I suggest he not bother making extra payments to pay off the mortgage before retirement. He can use the built-up equity for the new home purchase.

He needs to make sure he's maximizing his contributions to his 401(k) plan. Since he's 50, he can make catch-up contributions. I don't recommend he make post-tax contributions.

He should also start a 529 plan for Emma. In Pennsylvania, where he lives, contributions are tax-deductible for state income tax purposes, and the account grows completely tax-free. Withdrawals are also tax-free as long as they're used for post-secondary school education.

Whatever he has available after setting aside money for his 401(k) savings and his 529 plan can go into an investment account. Saving a lot will make his overall tax burden less onerous on his wealth; taxes on capital have dropped relative to taxes on income over the last 30 years in the U.S. One needs an income in order to develop capital, and the income is taxed right away, but Richard's dedication to saving will pay off.

Investment planning:

Richard is interested in a "growth" policy portfolio, and I agree that that policy is appropriate for him given his current situation, his goals, and how he responded to my questions. Here's the asset allocation I recommended for Richard:

Asset	Percent	Security
U.S. Stock Market	42%	DFA* Core Equity Fund
Large Cap Value	5%	DFA Large Cap Value
Small Cap Value	5%	DFA Small Cap Value

Foreign Stocks	18%	DFA International Core Equity
Emerging Markets	5%	DFA Emerging Markets Core Equity
Real Estate	5%	DFA Global Real Estate
I-T Fixed Income	6%	DFA Global Fixed Income
S-T Fixed Income	6%	DFA 2 YR Global Fixed Income
Inflation-Protected	6%	DFA Inflation-Protected Bond
Cash	2%	money funds

*DFA funds are only available through investment advisers.

All of these securities are mutual funds that passively invest in specific asset classes. Building a portfolio in this way will give Richard the best consistent returns, with lower volatility, expenses, and taxes. He'll likely have returns better than the vast majority of active managers, and he won't ever get hurt by trying to time the markets, which no one can do on a consistent basis. He also doesn't have to worry so much about underperformance or having returns far worse than the market, as some popular funds did in 2008 and 2009.

Having a pension really makes a difference in Richard's retirement planning. We don't know yet which option would make the most sense for him, but it seems likely that his pension can replace a very large chunk of his anticipated retirement expenses. When he's old enough to take it, Social Security will likely cover most of the rest. His savings and investments will then go towards making up the modest shortfall and providing a level of safety and security.

Emma's education still needs to be paid for, and it is still too far off to predict the exact age when Richard will be able to retire—but he's certainly on track to retire young.

Chapter 6

Investment Products

I've talked a lot here about investment products. If you're confused by the dazzling and ever-changing array of investment products, whether they're right for you, and how much they'll cost you, you're not alone. But here, as elsewhere, I find that the simplest approach usually works best. In this chapter, I'll briefly go over the key investment products and their costs.

Where do those costs come from? Most frequently, investing will have some combination of the following: sales commissions or loads to buy, sell, or hold the stock, bond, or fund paid to the brokerage company and the broker; fees for related investment advice; management fees and other costs for stock or bond funds paid to the fund company; and taxes paid to the appropriate governments. These costs vary wildly depending on the investment, and while cost is not the only factor that should go into your decision, strategically minimizing costs is a great way of maximizing your returns.

STOCKS

- What are they?

A share of common stock is an ownership interest in a corporation. Every corporation issues shares of stock when it comes into being, and each owner of shares has what is called an equity ownership interest in the issuing company. Each share represents an ownership interest equal to the share divided by the number of shares outstanding in the company.

Typically a small corporation issues 100 or 1,000 shares when it comes into existence, and most businesses stay small enough that they do not need to issue any more. Think of the small businesses in your neighborhood: many of them are corporations. Remember, not all corporations are the size of GE or Apple. But some rapidly-growing businesses get to the point where they cannot take advantage of all of the opportunities around them because they do not have enough money, or "capital." (Doesn't that sound like a fantastic problem? People want to buy more of your products or services than you can even provide!) Businesses raise capital by selling shares to either a small number of other investors in a private offering or placement, which is typically the first step, or to the public at large in what is called an Initial Public Offering (IPO).

Besides bringing money into the business, the owners who own shares before they are made available to the public get a chance to sell some of their shares. This is usually their first real chance to "cash in" on their fast-growing company. They can often realize a windfall and still be a relatively large shareholder.

- How do I buy them?

Once shares are available to the public, you can buy them through one of the larger stock exchanges like the New York Stock Exchange (NYSE), the NASDAQ, one of the smaller regional exchanges, or on the over-the-counter (OTC) market.

- How much do they cost?

If you buy or sell individual stocks there will be commission charges paid to the transacting broker for each transaction. Usually the transacting broker is also the custodian firm where you hold your shares, but it doesn't have to be. If you buy or sell stocks at an online or discount brokerage firm, the commission will probably be $10–$30. In the event that you use a full-service broker, the commission will be close to $1 per share for most types of accounts. The commissions may be less if you do frequent trading or if you have a big account.

There are no costs ordinarily associated with holding stocks, though some firms will charge account fees or low balance fees if you are below a minimum amount, typically a few thousand dollars for taxable accounts and $1,000 for IRAs. If you are opening an account without much money, you should inquire into these fees beforehand, but owning individual stocks doesn't make sense anyway if you have that little money because the costs are prohibitive.

If you have an investment advisor, it is likely that you will pay a small commission at a discount brokerage firm or mutual fund company, and in addition to those commission costs, you will pay fees to the advisor for the advice. Those fees will not be related to the specific purchase, and you will not likely owe them due to a specific transaction. They usually cover a specified time period, like a calendar quarter.

Most dividends you receive from the company are taxed for federal income tax purposes.

You don't pay any taxes for simply holding stocks, but you do if you sell them for a gain. You can hold stocks for 50 years; if they don't pay you a dividend, and you don't sell them, you will owe no federal taxes on them for that whole period.

When you sell a stock, you need to keep track of a few things for tax purposes: your cost basis in the stock, your proceeds from the sale of it, and the length of time you held it.

If you bought the stock, your cost basis is the total purchase price of the stock plus brokerage commissions and fees. If you received the shares from someone else as a gift, your cost basis is that of the person who gave you the shares, if they sold them for a gain, and the fair market value on the date you received them, if they sold them for a loss. If you inherited the shares, your cost basis is likely the value as of the date of death of the decedent (person who left you the stock), which is "stepped up" from the original cost basis of the decedent.

Your proceeds from the sale of stock are simply what you receive from the sale: the total amount you sold it for, minus any brokerage commissions and fees.

Your holding period begins when you acquire the shares by purchase and ends on the date you sell them. Gains or losses attributed to holding periods of one year or less are characterized as "short-term"; those for holding periods of longer than one year are "long-term." Shares that you have inherited are always considered long-term. Short-term gains are taxed at their marginal income tax rate; long-term gains are taxed at the applicable long-term capital gains tax rate.

- How do I make money?

You make money when the value of the stock you hold or sold is more than your cost basis in it. You also make money every time the stock pays you a dividend.

BONDS

- What are they?

Another option for a company when it wants to raise money (capital) is to issue bonds. Bonds are debt instruments of the issuing companies. American governments at all levels also issue bonds. Bonds are typically issued with face amounts of $1,000, which is what you pay for a new bond, and how much you will get back when it matures or is redeemed. There is also usually a coupon amount, which is the amount of interest you will receive for holding the bond, typically every six months for the life of the bond. A bond's yield is calculated by dividing the yearly coupon amount by the price of the bond. At issue, and upon redemption, the yield is the same as the stated coupon on the bond. There are also "zero-coupon" bonds, where you pay something less than the face amount. You don't get regular interest, but when they mature you get the face amount.

- How do I buy them?

Like stocks, most bonds are not purchased from the company that issues them. They are bought from other investors in the bond markets. If you don't buy bonds through a financial advisor, you could buy them through a brokerage firm. There, you'd buy either originally issued bonds or bonds already owned by other investors.

- How much do they cost?

Bond prices are quoted in terms of 100, so you can quickly calculate the price of multiple bonds, and it doesn't matter what the face amounts are in your calculations. Usually people buy and sell groups of multiple bonds in a transaction in the secondary markets. A bond with a $1,000 face value selling at 98, for example, is selling for $980 in the marketplace and is said to be selling at a discount. A $1,000 face-value bond selling at 102 costs $1,020 and is selling at a premium.

While the commissions on stock trades have gotten very cheap, those on bond trades have not yet. There is a lot of competition for stock trades, and so companies are constantly scrambling to give consumers better deals to lure their business. That is why there is an abundance of companies offering $10 (or cheaper) stock trades.

In the bond markets, you don't pay commissions. The bond dealers either mark down the price of the bond they are buying or mark up the price of the bond they are selling. The dealer makes money on the difference between what he buys and sells the bonds for, rather than a stated commission as a percentage.

- How do I make money?

Ordinarily, you make money when you receive your interest payment (usually every six months). In the case of zero-coupon bonds, you make money when the bond matures and you're paid its face value. Also, you can make money by selling bonds for more than you paid for them.

It's not easy to make money in the bond market for individual investors. I don't buy individual bonds for clients, but new clients will often hold them in the accounts they transfer to me. Whenever I have tried to sell clients' bonds for them, I have never gotten a quote from the custodial brokerage firm to buy a client's bond at or above the price listed on the client's monthly account statement or on the client's account on the custodian's website. That's right—never. Every time I have called, and this includes several brokerage firms, I have gotten a quote from $1 to $3 below the price that the custodian has valued the bond. That does not seem like a coincidence.

This pricing is part of the reason why I only recommend bond mutual funds or bond Exchange-Traded Funds (ETFs) for most individual investors. Individual retail investors have very little power in the bond market, and as you can see there is very little transparency in this market for ordinary investors. The hypothetical where the brokerage firm values its bond at 98 but is only willing to give you 95 for it is far too real.

Mutual Funds

- What are they?

A mutual fund is an investment company that pools the money of its shareholders to buy stocks or bonds, or other investment vehicles for its investors. I recommend that my clients buy funds that deal only with stocks or bonds, so those are the types of funds I'll discuss here.

Mutual funds are either open-ended or closed-ended. In open-ended mutual fund companies, which account for the vast majority of mutual funds, investors deposit money with the mutual fund company and receive shares in the mutual fund. All of the different investors who invest in a particular fund have their money pooled together.

The mutual fund manager takes all of this pooled money and uses it to buy the stocks or bonds for the fund. The price at which you buy shares of the mutual fund is called the Net Asset Value (NAV). The fund company calculates the NAV by dividing the total value of the pooled money by the number of shares outstanding. If you want to sell your shares, you sell them back to the company. Buying and selling is only done at the end of each trading day. You can put in an order to buy or sell at any time, and at the end of the day your order will be filled by the company at the NAV price at the close of business.

Closed-end mutual funds are bought and sold on the secondary markets, much like stocks and ETFs. You can buy them at any time during the trading day, and, as with stocks, prices are determined by the buyers and sellers in the marketplace. Closed-end funds usually sell at a discount to your NAV. For example, if the "ABC" closed-end mutual fund has an NAV of $10 per share, and the buyers and sellers in the marketplace are trading it at $9.50 per share, it is trading at a 5% discount to its NAV.

Brokers use that discount as a selling point to their customers. The customer actually has a chance to buy the fund at a discount to the underlying value of the shares. You really can buy the assets at a discount—much like buying a book and getting 5% off the regular price. The book has the same value; you can just take advantage of an opportunity to buy it more cheaply. Unfortunately, those types of funds almost *always* sell at a discount, so those intrinsic gains are usually never realized.

- How do I buy them?

You can buy no-load mutual funds directly from the mutual fund company, and you can usually buy most of those funds from discount brokerage firms. Some mutual funds are only sold through brokers, and others only through financial advisors.

- How much do they cost?

In every instance regarding a mutual fund, there will always be costs attributed to operating overhead, managing the investments, distributing and/or selling the fund, and for trading, which is the actual buying and selling of the investments within it. There might also be extra costs specifically paid to an outsider to sell the fund. These sales charges are called "loads," and they are paid to the advisors and brokers who sell the funds. The difference between a loaded fund and a no-load fund is whether someone is paid a commission to sell the fund. There are some companies who never pay sales loads, some who always do, and some who sometimes do.

The companies who sometimes charge a sales load usually use multiple sales channels to sell their funds. They might have a headquarters and a toll-free number you can call to buy their no-load fund, and they might also have advisors or brokers sell the same funds with a sales load. Some mutual funds also participate in arrangements where the broker charges the client a fee for the mutual funds they hold within a certain kind of account. The different types of fee arrangements can get pretty complicated and are outside the scope of this book.

- How do I make money?

Most mutual funds pay regular dividends and annual capital gains, so you will get a small ongoing return on your investment.

As for gains and losses, mutual funds are like stocks—if you hold or sell shares for more than you paid for them, including transaction costs, you have a gain. If your shares are worth less than what you paid for them or if you sell shares for less than your cost basis, you'll have a loss. The gain or loss will be long-term if held for a year and short-term if held for less.

Unlike with stocks, however, when you buy mutual funds, you'll have capital gains distributed to as your fund buys and sells companies. The more the fund buys and sells companies, the more likely it is that you'll receive these capital gains—which, unfortunately, are taxable. In fact, you might end up with more taxable gain from the fund's activity than you actually have in the fund—so it's possible you'll even have to pay taxes on funds that haven't actually been profitable for you.

This is another reason we like index funds—less buying and selling, and fewer capital gains. Index funds leave you with more control over when you'll have to pay taxes on your gains.

EXCHANGE-TRADED FUNDS

- What are they?

Like index mutual funds, exchange-traded funds (ETFs) are usually passively managed baskets of stocks or bonds, available in hundreds of varieties, covering most of the world's stock and bond markets. ETFs also compete with index mutual funds for being the lowest cost investment product available to consumers. We use these regularly in my firm, and I recommend some of them.

- How do I buy them?

These can be purchased at a brokerage firm or through your advisor. Like closed-end mutual funds, ETFs trade on stock exchanges and are bought and sold in the secondary markets. If you want to buy an ETF, you do not buy it from the issuer like you would an open-end mutual fund. Whether ETFs or index funds are cheaper depends upon the costs of the issuer and the amount that the buyer is going to buy. Most people of ordinary means will find index mutual funds cheaper than ETFs, but for large purchases ETFs will probably be cheaper.

Typically ETFs have lower internal expense ratios than the corresponding index mutual funds. However, when you buy or sell an ETF, you have to pay a commission to a brokerage firm, because ETFs are bought and sold on the exchanges. If you're buying $50,000 in shares and have to pay a $15 commission to the discount brokerage firm, that's probably the cheapest way to go. On the other hand, if you are buying $50 or $100 in your Roth IRA every month, obviously the commission will knock your transaction costs through the roof, and you'd be better off with the index mutual fund. (Those are extreme examples, but you get the point.)

The commission is a one-time charge and the internal expense ratios are ongoing—another consideration that may cause investors to lean toward ETFs.

- How much do they cost?

At most brokerage firms, the transaction costs of buying an ETF are about the same as those for a stock. Some newer ETFs trade without commissions. For consumers not using an advisor, you have to look at your potential purchases on an individual basis—both in terms of the current purchase you are contemplating and of your plan for the future. A good rule of thumb is to use mutual funds when you are dollar-cost averaging smaller amounts, like your 401(k) contributions, and ETFs with transaction charges when you are going to put a larger chunk of money to work right away. When I say larger amounts, the threshold in a lot of cases will be $5–10,000 or more.

The internal costs for ETFs are usually very low. Many are .25% per year or less.

- How do I make money?

You make money with ETFs in the exact same way as mutual funds.

SEPARATELY MANAGED ACCOUNTS AND HEDGE FUNDS

Separately managed accounts (SMAs) and hedge funds are hot-ticket items in the current investment world, but I don't recommend them to my clients for a number of reasons. SMAs are similar to mutual funds in that through an advisor, you pick a manager or a company for each style in which you want to invest (large-cap growth stocks, for instance), and someone from an investment company will manage your money in that style.

Why don't I recommend them? SMAs differ from mutual funds in one key regard—instead of owning the whole fund (or a couple of mutual funds), you individually own each and every stock and bond in the entire portfolio. For any security you sell during the tax year, you need to show on your tax return the cost basis, the purchase date, the sale date, and the proceeds of the sale, in addition to your gain or loss on *each security*. If you own six different portfolios with six different managers, and they each turn over 140 stocks in each of your portfolios, you need to show your gains and losses on 840 stocks or bonds! How long is that going to take your CPA to prepare, and at what cost? How big will your tax return be?

And that's not all—imagine the administrative hassle. Is it fun opening up a 120-page statement from your broker? Are you excited to know that you own three shares each in 500 different companies—all of which must be tracked? I think in this area the idea is much more appealing than the reality. Most of the clients I get who have these types of accounts cannot wait to get rid of them.

It's possible that hedge funds are even *more* popular than SMAs, but I don't recommend them either. Hedge funds are investments where investors pool their money into a single fund and a manager invests the money for their benefit. They are similar to mutual funds in many ways, but they're more exclusive in terms of who can invest in them and they're less restrictive in terms of how you can invest. Traditionally, hedge funds have been exclusively for "accredited investors," which is a fancy way of saying for people who meet certain income ($200,000 annually) or net worth ($1,000,000) requirements. For these investors who can seemingly afford to take the risk, the Securities and Exchange Commission (SEC) does not require the same types of disclosure necessary for mutual funds. Of course, these financial requirements have not kept pace with inflation. While it is still nice to be a millionaire or to make $200,000 annually, there are literally *millions* of people who meet these requirements, and many of them are not rich by any stretch of the imagination.

While I know that there are a lot of smart managers running hedge funds, I would advise most people to steer clear. First, there is not much disclosure to the investor. Lack of disclosure means you don't know what you're buying, and I am never comfortable with that. There are fewer restrictions on the manager than there would be in a mutual fund—so you may be interested in one style, and then the manager could change it after you have invested.

Hedge funds are among the most expensive investments in terms of costs and fees paid by the consumer. Hedge funds typically charge fees of 1–2% per year for managing the funds, which, while about the same as most mutual funds, is still too much. On top of that, the fund also keeps 15–20% of the profits it makes—or even more for the very popular funds. So with hedge funds, you have expensive products, you can't be quite sure what you are getting into, and you have to share 20% of the profits with the manager. Also, if you want to get out of most hedge funds, you need to wait at least one year from the time of your initial investment. Even after that, you can only withdraw your money at certain times, and with advance notice. It might also cost you a redemption fee.

Finally, hedge fund performance reporting is voluntary—meaning managers are only likely to tell you when the funds are making money. When they're losing? Well, that you'll most likely find out for yourself— the hard way.

INVESTMENT PLAN: JOHN AND SARAH

John and Sarah have a steady income and a lot of assets. John is 59, and Sarah is 58. They are in a good position to retire whenever they would like. However, their investment plan could use strengthening.

My plan:

John and Sarah indicated they were willing to have an aggressive portfolio and buy mostly stocks and stock funds. They have mostly individual stocks and less than ten percent of their portfolio is in bonds, so I would recommend bumping that up to 20% at this stage of their life. That is still more aggressive than I would typically recommend, but they are pretty comfortable with the risk and those assets are only about 20% of their overall net worth.

How does a 20% bond portfolio compare to an all-stock portfolio? According to statistics supplied by the mutual fund company Dimensional Fund Advisors (DFA), increasing a portfolio's bond component from 0% to 20% has historically decreased long-term annual returns from 12.5% to 11.9%, which is the downside of moving to more bonds. The upside is that the 20% bond portfolio decreased annualized standard deviation from 15.4% to 12.3%, which means that the portfolio is less volatile. In terms more people can understand, it also decreased the lowest one-year return from -48.4% to -37.7%. Those are pretty significant reductions in short- and intermediate-term risk.

Additionally, holding individual stocks, as opposed to stock funds, exposes you to a certain amount of uncompensated risk. The expected return of any individual stock is actually less than the expected return of the market in which it exists, because of the increased volatility and the fact that sometimes companies go bankrupt, destroying the shareholders' wealth. Because of that, there is no compelling reason to buy individual stocks, and I would recommend that John and Sarah sell theirs.

I recommend that John and Sarah's accounts be roughly 42% in a U.S. stock market fund, 5% in a large cap value fund, 5% in a small cap value fund, 17% in a developed international stock fund, 6% in an emerging market stock fund, 5% in a real estate fund, 9% in an intermediate-term bond fund, 9% in a short-term bond fund, and 2% in cash.

Because of their good-sized, tax-deferred (IRA) and taxable (brokerage) accounts, they have an opportunity to slightly increase their annual returns by correctly locating these assets within the different types of accounts they have. They can maximize their returns by moving the assets that pay a relatively high amount of their total return in the form of current interest or dividends into their tax-advantaged retirement accounts, and by moving the assets that pay less in interest and dividends into their taxable accounts.

This will decrease their taxes now and in the future, and can increase their after-tax returns by as much as .5% to 1% per year.

It decreases taxes now because assets that trigger a lot of taxes, like taxable bond funds, real estate, and large cap value funds, get put into accounts that don't face annual taxation, like IRAs and 401(k)s. It decreases taxes in the future because the assets that should increase the most through gains in capital, like the U.S. stock market fund and the small cap value fund, go into accounts that will be subject to long-term capital gains tax treatment, instead of just income tax treatment like 401(k) and IRA distributions. Currently, John and Sarah would pay long-term capital gains at the 15% rate and income tax at a 35% marginal rate.

For example, the small cap value fund will probably pay little or nothing in dividends most of the time, while the bond funds and real estate will pay a lot in dividends relative to their total returns. John and Sarah would start by putting real estate and taxable bond funds and large cap value funds in their IRAs, and then everything else into their brokerage account.

They have approximately $550,000 in their IRA accounts and $550,000 in their brokerage accounts. Using those approximations, they would need the following to build their $1,100,000 portfolio:

U.S. Stock Market	42%	$462,000
Large Cap Value	5%	$55,000
Small Cap Value	5%	$55,000
Developed Foreign	17%	$187,000
Emerging Markets	6%	$66,000

Global Real Estate	5%	$55,000
Intermediate Bonds	9%	$99,000
Short-Term Bonds	9%	$99,000
Cash	2%	$22,000

As I mentioned earlier, we can increase their expected returns by locating different funds within their brokerage and retirement accounts. This is what we'll buy in their brokerage account:

U.S. Stock Market	$462,000
Small Cap Value	$55,000
Intermediate-Term Bonds	$20,000
Cash	$13,000
Total	$550,000

This is what we we'll buy in their IRA accounts:

Large Cap Value	$55,000
Developed Foreign	$187,000
Emerging Markets	$66,000
Global Real Estate	$55,000
Intermediate-Term Bonds	$79,000
Short-Term Bonds	$99,000
Cash	$9,000
Total	$550,000

We'd buy regular taxable bonds in their IRA accounts because the dividend and gains won't be taxed on an annual basis. They just need to pay regular income taxes on whatever money they eventually take out of these types of accounts.

In the taxable brokerage account, we would buy a tax-free intermediate-term bond fund because they are in a high-income tax bracket.

Chapter 7

First Steps

We've covered what financial planning is, how to find the right planner, and what products your planner might suggest once you start working together. Now that you have the information you need to get started, I'll go into more in-depth coverage of the material your planner might go over with you. Being informed is the most important step toward making successful financial decisions. Of course, there's no way I can cover here everything your planner might bring up with you, or every factor that might be important to your situation. That's why it's so important to find a planner you're comfortable with and who works well with you.

Different planners have different approaches—your planner might skip some areas I'll cover here, and emphasize others that I don't focus on. That's totally fine. What's important is that she emphasizes your needs and understands your situation.

In this chapter, I'll cover cash flow planning and budgeting, insurance, investments, and income tax planning. In Chapter 8, I'll cover retirement planning, and in Chapter 9, I'll go over estate planning in-depth.

- Cash Flow Planning and Budgeting

The first step in cash flow planning and budgeting is creating a balance sheet and cash flow statement. You'll need both these documents to write your will as well and to assess whether you need life or disability insurance. You'll also use them to gauge your progress and determine whether you're saving enough and spending too much.

BALANCE SHEET

A balance sheet is just a snapshot of your wealth as of a particular day, and, unlike Enron, you won't have any off-balance sheet items. First, list all of your assets, like your house, savings accounts, and IRA. Estimate the value of anything that does not have a readily ascertainable value, such as your home. Add up all of these values. This total is the amount of your assets.

Separately, make a list of everything you owe. Include any mortgages, notes, credit card debts, or anything else that you owe to someone. Add these amounts, and this total is the amount of your liabilities. Subtract your liabilities from your assets, and you have your net worth.

SAMPLE BALANCE SHEET

Balance Sheet for John P. Client as of December 31, 2013

Assets:

Home	$600,000
Car	$35,000
Bank Account	$100,000
Rollover IRA	$600,000
Personal Items	$100,000
Assets	$1,435,000

Mortgage	$200,000
Car Loan	$20,000
Credit Cards	$25,000
Student Loans	$10,000
Liabilities	$255,000

Assets	$1,435,000
Liabilities	$255,000
Net Worth	$1,180,000

Why do you need a balance sheet? Well, for several reasons. The first is to get an idea of where you are on your road to wealth. Your balance sheet will tell you your net worth and serve as your starting point on the road to financial independence. You can check your progress at periodic intervals, such as once a year or once every five years.

It's also a good idea to periodically inventory what you own and see if it's still meeting your needs and performing adequately. You should look over your financial documents, insurance policies, contracts, estate planning documents, and any other similar items that seem pertinent.

Finally, documenting what you own is extremely useful for estate planning purposes. When you go to write your will, you will need to have a list of your assets so that you can make the proper decisions regarding their disposition at your death. Also, if your net worth is over a certain amount, you may need more than a simple will in order to pass your assets to your beneficiaries in a tax-efficient manner. Make a note of your ownership interest in each asset and any liabilities attached to it. You can lump everything together for your snapshot for financial planning purposes, but for estate planning purposes you need to know how you own your property, and if you're married, who owns what. Make a note of whether you or your spouse or partner own each item individually, and if you own anything jointly make a note of the type of ownership as well. I'll talk about this more in Chapter 10: Estate Planning.

Cash Flow Statement

A cash flow statement is simply a way of measuring your income and expenses over the period measured, usually a month, a quarter, or a year. List your income from all sources—salary, interest, dividends, rental property, etc.—and subtract from that all of your expenses over the same time period.

In order to account for short-term variances in either income or expenses, I recommend looking back over the last few months and the last year before estimating your future cash flows. Use your checkbook and bank statements to try to be as accurate as you can.

SAMPLE CASH FLOW STATEMENT

John P. Client Statement of Cash Flows for December 2013

Monthly Income:

Salary	$20,000
Interest from Savings	$75
Total Monthly Income	$20,075

Monthly Expenses:

Fixed Expenses

Mortgage + RE Taxes	$3,000
Utilities	$400
Food	$500
Clothing & Cleaning	$300
Payroll Taxes	$6,000
Medical/Dental	$500
Car Payment	$700
Life Insurance	$100
Property & Casualty	$250
Student Loans	$500
Savings	$2,000
Total Fixed Expenses	$14,250

Variable Expenses

Vacations/Travel	$500
Recreation/Entertainment	$300
Gifts	$200
Household Furnishings	$150
Credit Card Payments	$3,000
Total Variable Expenses	$4,150

Total Income	$20,075
Total Expenses	$18,550
Net Additional Savings (Borrowing)	$1,525

Your balance sheet will look different from your cash flow statement because the former is a snapshot of your wealth as of a certain date: a total of what you have accumulated. The latter is a measure of your current income and expenses and measures whether you are adding to your assets or are depleting them.

As with John, your savings should be at least ten percent of your gross monthly income. Saving money can be difficult for many people, but I've talked to countless good savers over the years, and they all have several habits in common—habits that you can learn, too. Many of them look at savings as paying themselves. They take the attitude that they are going to pay themselves first, and then with what's left over they pay bills or spend on discretionary items. That is why I pegged savings as a fixed expense. If you have never taken that approach, it is worth a try.

For example, because I know I have struggled in the past with saving, I have money automatically taken from my checking account and deposited into my various other savings, retirement, 529, and investment accounts. Instead of trying to be disciplined every month, I've created a system that does it for me.

While ten percent is a bare savings minimum, twenty percent is ideal. Your level of savings will largely determine how much you will accumulate during your lifetime for a given income level. Making more money and prudent investing can improve your situation, but unless you take the step of actually saving your money, you cannot begin to accumulate it.

I recommend the book *The Millionaire Next Door*, written by Dr. Thomas Stanley and published in 1996. The basic premise of that eye-opening book is that the majority of millionaires in the United States got where they are by working hard, saving diligently, and living below their means. Most wealthy people in America are not Lamborghini-driving rock stars or trust-fund babies, but people who worked hard and saved a lot of their money. For the most part they don't buy houses that they cannot afford, or spend huge sums on big car payments, or jet off to Aspen for the weekend. They are sensible and prudent and have a habit of saving, and after a lifetime of following these habits they have gained financial independence.

While I don't agree with all of Dr. Stanley's conclusions, the basic premise that most people gain financial independence by saving a lot is hard to dispute. If you are serious about following any of the advice in this book, the first thing you have to decide on is how much money you are going to save.

When estimating how much you need to save, I don't believe in making savings projections based on some far-off goal. If you are 30, and you are wondering how much you need to save for retirement, some number that you pull from a retirement calculator is unlikely to be accurate. You may get married or divorced or have eight children, or become fabulously successful, or do none of those things. You can be an entry-level employee at 30 and the CEO at 60. The projections from age 30 will be irrelevant. If you keep saving that $300 per month from age 30 and don't bump up the amount as your income increases, your lifestyle might take a big hit after you retire as CEO.

What you *can* decide to do is save 20% of your pay, no matter how much you are making. With that strategy, you're likely to be financially independent after a lifetime of saving—not that that is easy. Ten or 15 percent may be more realistic, and the percentage is likely to go up and down at various points in your life. Just remember that the more you save the more you will accumulate.

Financial planning is striking the right balance between living the kind of life you want to live and saving enough to gain your independence. You only get one bite at the apple, and it would be awful to go through life not experiencing anything just to meet your savings goals. Many of our parents and grandparents who were scarred by the Great Depression and two World Wars saved as though their life depended upon it—because at one time, it did.

We are fortunate to live in a place and a time where we have such freedom and opportunity. The idea that we can even have a conversation about the type of life we want to live is an alien concept throughout most of the human experience—even to most people alive today. Use your freedom and the opportunities around you to live the type of life you want to, but remember to save for the future.

CHAPTER 8

Planning for the Future

In this chapter, I'll discuss some of the various strategies you can use to prepare yourself for the future and offset any risks or unforeseen setbacks you may encounter.

- Insurance Planning and Risk Management

While there are numerous necessary forms of insurance, most advisors typically only concentrate on a few, like life, disability, and long-term care. You need to make sure that you have all of the right types of coverage and the right coverage amounts for your circumstances. You may need to have your advisor work in conjunction with your property and casualty agent to get this done.

Talk to your advisor and your property and casualty agent about the types and amounts of homeowners and auto insurance you should have given your personal circumstances and the area in which you live. You might not want to just try to get by with the minimum necessary by law. Often people do that because they are strapped for cash when buying their first new home or car, and then they never go back to see if their coverage is really appropriate. Now that you are taking the time to go over your financial situation, insurance coverage is an important part of that process. While you consider upgrading your coverage, it might be a good idea to increase your deductibles as well. Insurance should only be used when necessary, and having a high deductible might make you reconsider putting in a dinky claim. The money you save currently by increasing your deductible might even offset the costs of upgrading your coverage.

You should also talk to your advisor about getting umbrella coverage. Umbrella coverage increases the amount of personal liability coverage found in your auto and homeowners policies. This gives you higher protection, and that might be a good idea for you. These types of policies are usually pretty inexpensive.

If you do not currently have health insurance, or if you can actually make decisions about the coverage you have, talk to your advisor about what your options are.

Disability insurance is a type of insurance designed to compensate an insured person for a portion of his income lost because of a disabling illness or injury. If you or anyone else depends upon your ability to earn an income, you should probably have disability insurance. Most of the larger employers still offer this; most of the smaller ones don't. Many people are unaware of the need for this type of insurance, even though it is pretty likely that someone will suffer at least one disabling illness or injury during her working career.

The chance of becoming disabled for any length of time during a working career is somewhere around one in three for someone under 35. I don't know of very many people in their thirties or forties who could survive financially without their income for any real length of time. Disability insurance is a vital necessity for those people, and for other working people who are dependent upon or have someone else dependent upon their making a living.

Talk to your advisor about the type of coverage, the amount, and the elimination period that are right for you. These are all things that depend upon your situation.

If anyone else depends upon your income or assets for their financial support, you will need life insurance until you have enough assets to meet this potential need. If you just need coverage to provide assets for dependents, term insurance is the way to go. Term life insurance is simple and straightforward. Compared to other types of life insurance, it is very cheap. You select the coverage amount and the term, and pay the premium. It does not build up any kind of cash value, and when the term is over, so is the coverage.

The length of the term you should buy depends upon your circumstances. The term should certainly extend through the age of majority for your children, and maybe beyond, if one spouse earns significantly more than the other. Also, remember that even if one spouse is not a wage earner, that spouse still contributes in significant ways to the household, and should probably be insured. For instance, if you have children at home and a stay-at-home spouse, replacing the childcare and work around the house that your spouse provides would be more expensive than you might ordinarily think. You might have a hard time affording that expense without life insurance.

The other types of life insurance are generally referred to as permanent insurance. The major ones are whole life, universal, variable, and variable universal. Unlike term insurance, these types of insurance are not meant to end at a specific date in the near- to intermediate-term future. The coverage is much more expensive, and some of the excess cash builds value that you can use at a later date.

As I mentioned earlier, sometimes it might make sense to buy this type of insurance when your need for insurance is permanent, but generally I would avoid it for most people under most circumstances. Permanent insurance is much more expensive than term, and the cash values inside build up much more slowly than you ordinarily would through the use of other, more appropriate savings vehicles. I have run into too many people who say they have bought permanent coverage to fund some need other than the death benefit. Talk to your advisor about what is appropriate for your circumstances.

This is an area where it is particularly important for you to work with a fee-only advisor. There are potentially huge conflicts of interest here. Someone preparing your financial plan who's selling you insurance for commissions has a big incentive to steer you toward permanent insurance coverage. Remember, permanent coverage costs a multiple of the amount that term costs for the same coverage amount, and the commission as a percentage will also be several times the amount that the salesman gets for selling a term policy. That means that someone who sells you a permanent policy makes as much as 20 times more for selling you that policy instead of a term one. Most financial planners and experts agree that term makes the most sense for most situations, yet there is still a lot of permanent coverage sold every year. Wonder why?

As for how much coverage you need, the precise number would be the Net Present Value (NPV) of the future outlays that the coverage is intended to replace. That number is impossible to figure out because it isn't static, and no one really knows how much things will change when a loved one passes. The rule of thumb is usually eight to ten times your income, and you'll probably need more if you want to fully pay for private college tuition for more than a child or two.

Finally, long-term care insurance is coverage that includes a wide range of medical and support services for people with a degenerative condition, a prolonged illness, or a cognitive disorder. Long-term care is not necessarily medical care, but rather "custodial care," or providing an individual supervision or assistance with activities of daily living if they are cognitively impaired. As you can imagine, this type of insurance is becoming increasingly important as our lives keep getting longer and the costs of care keep increasing.

If you can afford coverage, it probably makes sense to discuss it with your advisor. Having a policy will make it more likely that you will be able to receive the care you need and may help you save assets for your heirs.

- Employee Benefits Planning

If you receive any benefits as a condition of your employment, your advisor can help you to evaluate them and choose the ones that work best for you. Most benefit plans include sick time and vacation days, some of the forms of life, disability and health insurance previously discussed, and a way to save for retirement.

A generation or two ago, most employees that worked for large employers had some sort of defined benefit pension. Based on your salary, age, and years of employment, upon retirement you would get a benefit that lasted until you died. It's not breaking news that those plans aren't too popular anymore. If you have one, congratulations!

If employees have a retirement plan at work these days, it is most likely a 401(k) if they work for a large or medium-sized employer, a 403(b) if they work for a non-profit, and a Simplified Employee Pension Plan (SEP-IRA) if they are self-employed or work for a small employer.

The success of these plans depends on employees contributing a sufficient amount to their plans and picking the right investments. Unfortunately, most employees cannot afford to save enough, and many don't know which investments to pick.

I often see prospective clients who have chosen multiples of the same types of funds, not realizing that they aren't actually diversifying their accounts by picking three large cap growth funds. Even more frequently, I see people who have just kept all of their money in the cash option.

• Investment Planning

Your advisor will analyze your investments and determine the best course of action for you to take. Often advisors will suggest big changes in this area, usually because clients either do a poor job of diversifying, or because the client had selected investments over time with no clear plan or purpose other than hoping to make a profit.

Your advisor will suggest an asset allocation for all of your investments. This breaks down how much you should put in stocks versus bonds, and how much should go into each subset of the major asset classes. If you are just using your advisor for your financial plan, you will need to make the changes on your own. If you are going to stick with your advisor for ongoing investment advice, he will make the changes.

If you choose the ongoing advice route, you and your advisor will need to craft an Investment Policy Statement (IPS). Your IPS spells out how he will manage your assets. It will go beyond simple asset allocation to list what your advisor is allowed to do and what he is prohibited from doing. The benefit of an IPS is that it establishes a clearly-written plan for how he will manage your investments—you should never be surprised.

In the IPS, your advisor should also spell out what kind of tools he will use to implement your plan. Most advisors use some sort of mix of mutual funds and exchange-traded funds (ETFs), individual stocks and bonds, separately managed accounts (SMAs), and hedge funds (the latter, only if the client is wealthy enough.)

Your advisor will also spell out whether he uses active or passive management or some mix of the two. As I said previously, my firm uses passive management, which is in the minority, but growing rapidly. Most advisors use active management. Many do a mix of the two, because they think some markets are more efficient than others. For example, some advisors may use passive management for large U.S. stocks because they think it is a heavily analyzed and traded part of the market; therefore it's less likely that these stocks will outperform the market. These advisors will use active management for smaller stocks and foreign or emerging market stocks, because they think those markets aren't analyzed and traded as much and therefore may provide more opportunities for them to show their skill in picking stocks or funds. I don't agree with that thinking, but it's fairly common.

It bears repeating that it is not part of your advisor's job to pick market-beating returns. That is not his value proposition, and you will pay a lot more looking for active managers who try to beat your respective indices, in terms of management expenses, trading costs, and possibly, taxes. You have no way of knowing in advance whether it will work. You do know for sure that your managers will be saddled with the extra costs as they attempt to beat your market indices.

Don't work with an advisor who tries to sell you on the fact that he can beat the markets or choose managers who can. He is either being untruthful or he might not really understand how markets work. Your advisor can show you that in the *past* his investment returns compare favorably to some index or other, but as you know, past performance is not a guarantee of future results.

- Income Tax Planning

How your advisor works with you in regard to income tax planning depends upon several factors, such as how complex your situation is and the level of training and sophistication your advisor has in tax planning.

If your advisor is a CPA who is also going to prepare your tax return, and you are a business owner with numerous types of investments, obviously your advisor will wade pretty deeply into your planning and income tax return. If you are a wage earner with limited investments and possible deductions, there is not a lot for the advisor to do in any event.

In most cases, there is usually more of a middle ground. Your advisor will look at your tax return and make some suggestions for you or your CPA to consider. These suggestions will typically relate to retirement plan contributions or realizing gains or losses from stock sales to best take advantage of your current situation with losses you have carried forward on your tax return, or with unrealized gains and losses you have on stocks or funds in your portfolio. Of course, there are many other things that are possible; these are what I have seen most from my vantage point.

INVESTMENT PLAN: RAY AND SUSAN

Ray and Susan are both 55 and would like to retire at age 60. Their combined taxable income is about $206,000 per year. They have a mortgage, which will be paid off in about six years based on their current payment plan. Their only other debt is a car loan. Susan has a 401(k) with her employer, and Ray has a 403(b) with his.

My plan:

Susan and Ray are already saving, but after looking over their finances, they decided they were able to save an additional $6,000 per year. The best way to do that is to increase Ray's 403(b) contributions. Since their taxable income puts them in the 33% marginal income tax bracket, if they elect to put away $9,000, they will save $2,970 in federal taxes, and their net income will only go down by $6,030.

I'd encourage Susan and Ray to pay off their mortgage sooner. Once their mortgage is paid off, that frees up more than $1,000 per month in principal and interest. (Unfortunately, they still need to pay RE taxes!) They can save that amount until their money market savings is up to $50,000. Any gifts or other extra money should go in that account, too.

Once the money market is up to $50,000, they can shift some of those previous mortgage and interest payments to maximize the contributions to Ray's 403b, and whatever is left over then should go into the money market fund.

Once the money market fund gets to $100,000, and they are both maximizing their retirement plan contributions, it will be time to open a brokerage account and invest it according to my investment plan below.

After they pay off their house, they can set up their checking account so that the amounts of their mortgage and interest are automatically transferred monthly to their money market fund. As I've said before, the more we automate savings and investments in our lives, the better our outcomes.

In order for them to both retire at 60 with a standard of living approaching what they have now, they will need to save *a lot* over the next five years. But some people are choosing another option: instead of saving extra in order to retire sooner, they're using surplus income to do what they'd like to do now, and continuing to work longer. Rather than trying to save $40–50,000 a year for the next five years, Susan and Ray could take a great trip or two every year, splurge on a new car or boat—whatever they're most interested in—and work an extra couple of years before retiring. Of course, this option depends on your ability to continue working. At some point, most people either *have* to retire or really, really want to. You will know that you can afford to retire when your cash flow from social security, pensions, retirement accounts, and investment accounts can support your lifestyle indefinitely. (I know that sounds obvious, but most people never put that together until they think about actually retiring.)

Investment plan:

Given Ray and Susan's situation, I think a balanced "growth and income" investment policy would be appropriate for the next five to seven years at least.

Susan has two good options for her 401(k). The first is to switch all of the current investments and all of the new contributions to 40% S&P 500 Index fund; 10% Russell 2000 Index fund; 20% EAFE Index fund; and 30% Aggregate Bond Index fund, and re-balance yearly back to those targets until she retires. A lot of plans will re-balance automatically for you on your birthday or some other date you or they specify.

A less ideal, but much simpler option for her would be to choose the target-date fund in her plan that most closely aligns with the fund allocation I have chosen for her, which in her case would be the 2025 fund. The target-date fund buys several funds within the fund and invests them for you in a portfolio that gets more conservative over time. I think most are a little more conservative than they should be, so that's why I am recommending a fund for her with a target date several years beyond when she will retire.

Ray has similar options for his 403(b). The best option would be to put 40% in the Large Cap Index; 10% in the Small Cap Index; 20% in the International Index; and 30% in the Global Bond portfolio. Otherwise, he could put it all in the Target 2025 fund his plan offers.

Susan's prior 401(k) should be combined in an IRA rollover with the account that is currently at TD Ameritrade. Those assets and Ray's SEP-IRA should be invested as follows:

Asset	Percent	Security
U.S. Stock Market	34%	DFA Core Equity
Large Cap Value	4%	DFA Large Cap Value
Small Cap Value	4%	DFA Small Cap Value
Foreign Stocks	13%	DFA International Core Equity
Emerging Markets	5%	DFA Emerging Markets Core Equity
Real Estate	5%	DFA Global Real Estate
I-T Fixed Income	10%	DFA 5 YR Global Fixed Income
S-T Fixed Income	10%	DFA 2 YR Global Fixed Income
Inflation-Protected	10%	DFA Inflation-Protected Bond
Money Market	5%	

Since all of their accounts are IRAs, we don't need to worry about where we locate assets for tax purposes. All we try to do is make sure all of the funds fit into their accounts without having to make too many duplicates.

CHAPTER 9

Retirement Planning

Retirement planning can really be seen as the crux of financial planning. Being able to retire means that you are financially independent and don't need a job or anyone else to support you.

The biggest part of my job is helping people plan for their retirement; that is, figuring out whether their pension, Social Security, retirement plans, savings and investments is enough to last them the rest of their life. This isn't an area where "good enough" is good enough. I don't like to see someone retire unless their odds of success are more than 90% according to the current thinking within the financial planning community. We can never be 100% sure of success, because life is too filled with uncertainty. But if they start out with a 90% chance, stay cognizant of their circumstances, and make adjustments along the way, they are likely to be fine.

If you're between 55 and 65 or thereabouts, you're probably starting to think about retirement. You're looking forward to a time when you can relax, pursue hobbies or passions, and reap the rewards of a lifetime of work and savings. But do you have enough to see you through? How do you know when you do? In this chapter, I'll talk about how to answer those questions and outline three strategies to successfully set up your retirement plan:

- **Strategy #1**: The way to assess just how much you need for retirement—in solid, dollars-and-cents terms.

- **Strategy #2**: How to get more out of Social Security—actions (and their timing) that you may not have thought about but which can substantially increase your retirement income.

- **Strategy #3:** Knowing how to "cash out" your assets for best returns—which ones to sell, which ones you'll want to hang onto, and why.

RETIREMENT FUNDING—HOW MUCH IS ENOUGH?

The number one question everyone has about retirement is, "How much money do I actually need?" And the number one answer to that is, "You can't hit a target you can't see." So let's talk about how to make that target more visible.

That can be easier said than done, of course. The amount of money you'll need to retire is a moving target, dependent on all kinds of variables. But there is a way to determine what you need, and it's accurate for many investors.

Step #1:

Calculate how much you need to live in your first year of retirement. As a rule of thumb, many middle-income and upper-middle-income retirees can expect to live off between 70 and 80 percent of their current income. Wealthier people usually need to live off of a smaller percentage of their pre-retirement income. Of course, what you need could be very different. You need to get a sense of what you will expect to spend.

So for example, if your family makes $100,000 a year, you might expect to need about $75,000 to maintain your current lifestyle while in retirement.

Step #2:

Now, take that annual income needed figure for the first year and divide it by 4%.

In our example, then, you'd take $75,000 and divide it by four percent. The result is $1.875 million. For many people out there, this figure is what they'll need to retire and maintain their current standard of living.

Does that figure seem insurmountable? Or at least distant? Don't let it throw you; this calculation is a raw figure that doesn't take into account anything from Social Security, a pension, or any other outside source of income. Since most people will have those alternate sources, let's look at those, too.

Back to our hypothetical example:

Let's say you need $75,000 (inflation adjusted) per year to maintain your current lifestyle in retirement, but that you expect to receive $20,000 per year in Social Security payments. That means you'll need only $55,000 per year (inflation adjusted) to achieve your retirement lifestyle. Multiplied out by our 4% figure, that brings your estimated retirement needs down to $1.375 million, a full half-million dollars less!

Social Security benefits can be a big plus in your retirement plans—and even bigger if you know how to get the most out of them.

How to Get the Most from Social Security

Social Security isn't the be-all and end-all of your retirement income; it's not going to provide your entire retirement nest egg, nor was it ever meant to. But it *can* help reduce the amount of resources you need to accumulate from other sources in order to have a comfortable retirement... and by more than you might expect.

First, think about your own potential lifespan. I'm not trying to be morbid here—but if your family is full of octogenarians and older, you're very likely to live a good, long time. Which means you'll want to think in terms of claiming your benefits *later* rather than sooner. How does that break down in dollars and cents?

If you're married, you can use one strategy: one spouse claims early at 62 to 66, while the older, higher wage earner waits as long as possible to collect at 66 to 70. This pays off because of the Social Security rules and joint life expectancy.

We all know it's good to wait to claim Social Security until you're past "minimum" retirement age. If you claim benefits at 62, you'll get only 75% of your full retirement age benefits. But for each year you wait past 66, you get 8% *more* (plus an inflation adjustment). This means that your maximum benefit at age 70 is actually equal to *132%* of the full retirement-age payout.

How does this happen? Well, because these adjustments are supposed to be actuarially neutral, but they're really not. That is because married couples get a special deal: when one dies, the survivor can take the dead spouse's benefits (if they're higher) and drop his or her own. So often, one spouse claims early, between ages 62 and 66, while the higher wage-earner waits to collect. That way, the payout is bigger overall, for a longer period of time.

Part of why this system works the way it does is joint mortality. To illustrate this, let's consider a husband and wife both born on Jan. 1, 1950. When they become eligible for Social Security at 62, the wife will have a projected life expectancy of 84 years and 8 months, while the husband's will be 81 years and 10 months. But according to the Government Accountability Office (GAO), there's a 50% chance one spouse will die before age 78, and a 50% chance the second will hold on until almost age 89.

So, in effect, a woman who takes Social Security at 62 isn't necessarily accepting a smaller payout until 84, but only (on average) until her husband (or she) dies prior to age 78. As for that bigger check that the husband waits until 70 to get? Half the time, it will keep coming to one of them for 19 years or more.

Keep in mind, though, that these are only actuarial averages. That's why a glance at your heredity isn't a bad idea. If there are inherited diseases or disorders that affect one or the other of you, or if either of you is in any kind of high-risk situation—say, once you retire you're going to take advantage of that urge to learn to sky-dive!—all bets may be off. This strategy doesn't work if you both die really young (when benefits at 62 would have worked best) or live for an especially long time (where 70 would be best). Nevertheless, Social Security can be a big help toward feathering that retirement nest.

This is only one strategy. You need to talk to your advisor about what may be best for you.

Using Assets to Enhance Your Retirement Nest Egg

You can start taking money from your retirement accounts without penalty at 59½. But just because you can doesn't mean you *should*. Often, you should spend non-retirement accounts first. Why?

You'll benefit from lower current taxes. Taxable account assets may qualify for long-term capital gain rates, usually 15%, and that tax is only on gains. All withdrawals from retirement accounts, however, are taxable at ordinary rates, which go up to 35%.

You'll enjoy continued tax-deferred growth. Spending taxable accounts first allows your retirement account to keep growing, free from current taxation.

You'll leave more for your heirs. Leaving an IRA lets heirs continue the tax-deferred ride. With a "stretch" IRA, beneficiaries withdraw from the account over their life expectancies.

You're going to tap other assets besides retirement funds for the tax and legacy benefits. But which ones should you tap first? Selling stock or bond positions that are bigger than their target allocations both frees cash and keeps you diversified.

Concentrated holdings

Trim concentrated holdings, especially your employer's stock. If that stock's in a company retirement plan, consider taking the shares out of the plan when you leave the firm, using Net Unrealized Appreciation

(NUA) rules. You'll pay income tax on the cost basis, but all of the prior appreciation will be taxed at long-term capital gain rates, which can result in substantial savings. A caveat: NUA rules are very specific, so get professional advice first.

Highly-appreciated assets

You can leave taxable assets to heirs; your basis is normally stepped up to the value on the date of your death, which eliminates the capital gains tax on appreciation during your lifetime. Highly appreciated assets also make good charitable gifts, because you can deduct their fair market value when they're donated. If you anticipate estate taxes, keep some taxable assets to cover the bill; otherwise, your heirs might have to raid your retirement account, which will then trigger additional income tax.

Putting it All Together

If the biggest shortcoming many people face when approaching retirement is ignorance about what they have, the second-biggest is not having a plan. Fortunately, it's easy to fix both of these flaws and give yourself a lot more security in the process by using the experience and expertise of a financial planner to help you map everything out. Professional help can take the stress out of these decisions and make them as worry-free as possible, even in the volatile economies we've seen over the last couple of generations.

It just takes a little upfront work and guidance now to make sure you enjoy the future for which you've worked hard all your life. When it comes to the future, every day counts. So make today the day you take charge of that future, and relax for the tomorrows to come.

CHAPTER 10

Estate Planning

We've covered a lot of ground in the last nine chapters, but we're not quite done yet. You know about the different kinds of financial planners and financial products, you've figured out your net worth, and you've started thinking about retirement. You might have even already found the perfect financial planner for your needs and goals. Congratulations! But you're not quite done yet: you need to get your legal documents in order. Some documents are so critical that everyone—and I mean everyone—needs them. Estate planning is of the utmost importance—I simply can't emphasize it enough.

To draw up the necessary legal documents, you need to see a lawyer. Only a lawyer can draw up legal documents. Don't trust any non-lawyer who says they can provide them for you. It is common practice for many financial planners to ask to review these documents for you. While they may mean well, if they are not lawyers they do not necessarily know what they should be looking for other than to see that you have the documents in place. Of course, you may not be able to tell that either. Most good lawyers who do not practice estate planning law will not even write wills for themselves!

Some people advocate using computer software to write your estate planning documents. There is cheap legal software out there that seems pretty good and is fairly easy to use. Should you use it? I would advise against it. How do you know that the law hasn't changed since the software was written? How do you know that your situation fits exactly into those incorporated within the software? The software will guide you down a single path by asking you specific questions as you fill out forms. What if there is something outside that narrow path that would make you really, really happy? You'll never know, because your needs are outside the program's scope.

Every so often you see some statistic about the number of adults walking around without a will. I have seen estimates ranging from 40–70%. Don't be one of them! It will cost between a few hundred and a few thousand dollars to get all of the estate planning documents you will need. But that small investment is hugely important. In this chapter, I'll talk about wills, trusts, and powers of attorney.

WILLS

Let me say it again: a will is absolutely essential. When you pass away, do you want the government to divvy up your property and decide who has custody of your children? If your answer is "No," you need a will.

Dying without a will is called "dying intestate," and it means you cannot select the beneficiaries of your estate; make gifts to specific friends, family members, or charities; name the executor of your estate; or designate a guardian for your minor children.

Your heirs will suffer multiple consequences: your federal estate taxes may be much higher without properly using the credit to which you're entitled, or any other tax-saving devices; your state death taxes may be higher; your probate expenses will generally be higher; and a *court may decide who raises your children!* Your state government has set out rules that further specify what happens to your estate if you die without a will. They are called the rules of intestate succession.

Avoiding these negative consequences is simple: all you need is a will. If you don't know where to start, ask other professionals or colleagues to refer you to a good estate planning attorney; you can also ask friends or acquaintances, if you're comfortable. Your local bar association probably has a referrals system as well.

A good lawyer will take some time to explain the process and will clearly spell out the fees involved. Ask how the process works and don't be afraid to ask him to clarify anything you don't understand. You aren't going to be able to figure out whether he is a mediocre lawyer or a great lawyer because you don't have the knowledge or experience to judge his expertise. What you can figure out is whether he will clearly answer your questions, whether you wouldn't mind spending a few hours with him (because you will have to), whether you trust him, and whether you would be comfortable calling him in the future if you have further questions, or when your documents need revising.

You'll need to name an executor for your will. The executor is the person you put in charge of seeing that the terms of your will are met. If you have minor children, you need to name a guardian who will care for them after your death. If you are going to have testamentary trusts (i.e. trusts emanating from your will), you will need trustees to be responsible for their administration.

You should have backups for all of these positions in case the originals are unwilling or unable to act when the time arises. You'll also want to confirm that the people you name are willing to take on these responsibilities. All of these roles require a good deal of commitment, and they are very important to you. You should have someone who is up for the task. Asking someone to care for your children after your death is quite a request—don't spring it on anyone! You should talk through these issues with your spouse or partner, and take the time to determine who will suit your needs best.

The terms of your will necessitate a balance between control of where your assets are allocated and taxation of those assets. If you don't want taxes, you have to give up control. If you want control, you have to pay taxes. At the extremes, this is easy to see. If you want to control exactly how your assets are disposed of in your will, you can. Unfortunately, you'll probably be subjected to the highest taxes. At the other side of the spectrum, if you follow the dictates of the tax code, you can certainly decrease your taxes to a minimal amount or percentage—but you won't be able to keep complete control over your money. You need to give up some control in order to decrease your taxes.

A good lawyer will balance these competing interests in the way that is most satisfactory to you. Minimization of estate taxes is a major goal of estate planning, but it is not the only one. You have to let your lawyer know what you want and how important each of your goals is to you.

If your lawyer recommends any estate-planning vehicles in your will in order to save money on taxes, such as a disclaimer trust or a credit shelter trust, you will have some other considerations. This will be more likely as you cross the threshold amount of assets that get taxed by the federal government, which is currently $5,340,000 per person in 2014. You have to make sure that your lawyer is trying to meet your needs and fulfill your wishes as best as he can, considering the constraints of the tax system.

In most jurisdictions, most married couples own property as Joint Tenants with Rights of Survivorship (JTWROS), also called Tenancy by the Entireties (ATBE) in some jurisdictions. This type of property passes automatically to the other owner at one owner's death. While it is a fairly common ownership type, if you have substantial enough assets to be concerned with estate and gift taxes, your lawyer may suggest that you re-title some of your assets as part of your estate plan.

Though it is less popular, another fairly common way of owning property is as Tenants in Common (TIC). As a Tenant in Common, you own a specific fractional share that does not automatically go to the other owner(s) at your death. You can sell it or leave it to someone else besides the other owner(s).

Besides these, there are other ways of owning property as an individual, and of course, you can also own shares in a partnership or a corporation, or any of the newer hybrids of these forms. Make a note of your ownership interest and make sure the lawyer who drafts your will is aware of it as well. Your lawyer will need this when drafting estate planning documents that best suit your needs and goals.

ESTATE TAXES

I won't go too much into the issue of estate taxes here—a lawyer will tell you what works best for you depending on your circumstances and the state in which you live, and whole books have been written on the subject of estate taxes!

As the name implies, the Federal Estate and Gift Tax is the group of federal statutes used to collect taxes when people give gifts of money or property, both while they are alive and when they die. It is not an inheritance tax, which taxes you on receipt of an inheritance and is paid by the recipient. Rather, it is collected from the estate of the descendant. Most gifts are not subject to gift tax, and most estates are not subject to estate tax. Despite the continuing outcry over "death" taxes, and legislation to abolish them, only a very small fraction of one percent of taxpayers' estates are subject to the tax.

Estate taxes and gift taxes work in conjunction. Each donor may give away up to $14,000 per year during her lifetime to each beneficiary (donee), and she is allowed to give that much to as many beneficiaries as she likes. Upon death, each decedent is allowed to transfer $5,340,000 free of estate taxes. Any gifts you make in your lifetime above the Annual Gift Tax exclusion go against your unified credit. The unified credit is basically the amount of tax that corresponds to the exemption amount.

When someone dies, everything they own, minus whatever they owe on it, becomes their gross estate. There are some deductions available for certain expenses. Whatever is left over is called the taxable estate. The marginal tax rate is applied to the taxable estate to come up with the tentative tax, and the unified credit is applied to the tentative tax. If the tentative tax is greater than the unified credit, the tax due is the difference. If the tentative tax is less than the unified credit, no tax is due.

In 2014, the estate-death-time-transfer exemption amount is $5,340,000. That means a couple can effectively shield up to $10,680,000 pretty easily.

LARGER ESTATES

If you are close to the limit, or might reasonably be by the time of your death, or have any concerns that the estate tax exemptions might actually go down for a change, your lawyer will probably suggest some type of advanced estate planning. As I said, disclaimer trusts and credit shelter trusts are very common.

If you accumulate enough assets to go comfortably beyond these exemption amounts, the next estate-planning vehicle is usually the Irrevocable Life Insurance Trust (ILIT). Normally, the amount of life insurance you own at the time of your death is included in your gross estate.

However, you can gift life insurance to a trust, and if you do it properly, the death benefit goes to your heirs exempt from estate taxes. The gift is usually made in the form of the annual premium for the insurance. The gifts are irrevocable, meaning once you make them, you can't take them back, and the amounts are subject to the annual gift tax exclusions. Of course, you need to be able to qualify for life insurance, and it needs to fit in with your overall plan. I see these used quite a bit.

For other people who have accumulated estates over the threshold amounts, a common estate-planning technique is the use of limited partnerships, sometimes called Family Limited Partnerships (FLPs), because most or all of the partners are related. A person or couple with multiple real estate or business interests can transfer all their interests into a limited partnership. The person doing the estate planning will be the general partner, and his ultimate beneficiaries will be the limited partners. Each year the general partner will use his annual gift exclusion amount to make gifts to each of the limited partners.

Because of the structure of the partnership, the general partner can more efficiently pass his assets to his intended beneficiaries. He can move them more easily and more fairly to his beneficiaries because he is not trying to give fractional shares of different individual assets to his different family members; rather, he is giving a fraction of the entire entity. He can also keep control over how the assets are managed even after making the gifts.

From a tax standpoint, he can discount the amount of his gifts each year (and this is okay with the IRS) because the limited partners have a limited ability to dispose of their gifts. Because the limited partners cannot easily sell their shares in the limited partnership, their interests lack marketability and liquidity. Also, because they have no voice in the management of the company, their shares are worth less than if they had a controlling interest.

In addition to lawyers to draw up these partnership agreements, you will need valuation experts and CPAs. These experts will evaluate the property to determine its value and how much of a discount is reasonable. This discount is very valuable because it allows you to pass more assets tax-free. If your assets are discounted 25%, that means you can pass one-fourth more than you would be able to tax-free without the discount. Instead of passing $14,000 per year per beneficiary, you would be able to pass $18,620. That amount can really add up.

These partnerships can also help protect your assets from judgments and creditors; you don't have to worry about undue influence from your child's spouse, or losing family control if your children get divorced. You can continue to manage the properties as you see fit.

These are not cheap to set up, but if they are done properly they can be very valuable. You need to speak to an attorney to see if one is right for you.

TRUSTS

In addition to the aforementioned testamentary trusts, there are revocable *inter vivos* trusts, also called living trusts. Living trusts are not set up to avoid estate taxes, but to protect your assets and keep them out of probate when you die.

The person who sets up a living trust is called the grantor; the person who oversees the trust is the trustee; and the person who receives distributions from it is the beneficiary. Often for living trusts, these three people are one and the same. There is also a remainder beneficiary who receives distributions from the trust once the primary beneficiary dies.

You will need to hire a lawyer to draw up the necessary legal documents. (There is software that you can use, but you already know how I feel about that—don't do it!) You will also have to transfer ownership of your assets into the trust. Once you have done that, going forward you would use the trust to buy whatever it is you will be accumulating: real estate, stocks, bonds, etc.

If privacy is a big concern of yours, a living trust may help. When your will is probated, it is there for the world to see. People might not exactly camp out at the courthouse to be the first to see the probated will of Joe Sixpack, but if you place a high value on your privacy, a living trust might be preferable for you. No outsider can see the contents of your trust.

A living trust can also potentially shield your assets from creditors, as long as the trust wasn't created specifically to defraud them. Some of our clients who have careers with a high risk of liability (doctors, for example) use living trusts more frequently.

There are no estate tax savings in using a living trust, but you can avoid probate, and in some states, probate is an expensive proposition. If you live in a state that charges probate fees as a percentage of your assets that go through probate, a living trust is probably desirable and necessary, and worth the cost if you have sufficient assets.

Some proponents of using living trusts argue that almost everyone should have them, but I am not one of those people. Certainly, if probate would cost you more than the time and money it takes to set up and administer a trust, go for it. But trusts are not the panacea some zealots claim. Your estate planning attorney will help you determine whether a trust is a good fit for your needs.

DURABLE POWER OF ATTORNEY

A power of attorney authorizes someone to act on your behalf. A "durable" power of attorney remains in effect even if the grantor of the power becomes incapacitated. It only terminates when the grantor revokes it or dies. A durable power of attorney designates the person who can execute legal documents or make financial decisions for you in the event you become incapacitated.

Typically, these involve spousal relationships, or relationships between a parent and his/her adult child. The agent, or person who has the power to act, owes the grantor a legal fiduciary duty to act in the grantor's best interests, because the agent is in a position to be able to do great harm to the grantor. Obviously, trust is a big factor here. You don't grant the guy down the street a durable power of attorney to act for you.

Durable powers of attorney should only be drafted by a lawyer.

HEALTHCARE POWER OF ATTORNEY (OR PROXY) AND LIVING WILL

A healthcare power of attorney (or proxy) authorizes someone to make medical decisions for you when you are unable to do so. A living will establishes whether you want your life to be sustained by certain artificial means in the event that you are in a terminal condition or a persistent vegetative state. An advanced directive is a document that incorporates both forms. These documents are incredibly important—they make your wishes clear. These documents are also very important for your loved ones. You don't want to leave the awful decision to maintain or end life support in someone else's hands. Your friends and family will be devastated enough without having to feel all of the emotions involved in making such a life-altering decision.

After your attorney has drawn up the appropriate documents, you need to make sure that they are in the right place so that they will be effective for you and can be followed if possible. Talk to your attorney about which specific documents you need in your jurisdiction.

CONCLUSION

We've covered a tremendous amount of ground together: we've discussed what on earth it is a financial planner actually does, the different types of financial planners and advisors and how to find the right planner for you, and how much good financial advice will cost you. We've talked about how to make sure the independent advisory mold you've chosen is a good fit for your dreams, goals, and individual situation, and why it's so important to recognize that there's no single advising mold that fits everyone's needs. I've gone through the qualifications your advisor should have and walked you through the six steps of the financial planning process in detail. We've gone over the basic financial products, their advantages, and their disadvantages, and how to put them to work for you. We've looked at the fundamentals of planning for the future and preparing for a successful, comfortable retirement, and finally, I've given you an overview of estate planning.

The more educated you are about financial planning, the better prepared you'll be to make good decisions and plan for your future. But if there's one single thing I want you to take away from this book, it's this: you don't have to go it alone. An independent financial advisor is the best ally you can have as you look forward to the future. As an advisor, it's my job to work directly with my clients to ensure they set—and reach—realistic goals, make their assets work for them, and develop a clear, comprehensive plan for growing their assets and savings. The goal of this book is not to set you adrift in a sea of information that you don't have the time to wade through; instead, I'm here to give you the information you need to select the best possible financial advisor for your needs and ensure he's working for you in a way that matches your goals and expectations.

In my years as a financial planner, I've worked with about as broad a spectrum of clients as you can imagine, and I can tell you that the people who are most successful in meeting their goals are often the same people who understand that, while it's important to be educated about the financial planning process, it's equally important to view your advisor as an ally and an advocate. Remember, this is your future we're talking about here—don't shortchange yourself by settling for an advisor who doesn't mesh with your needs. Your relationship should be positive, inspiring, and profitable, and your advisor should be able to meet you where you're at—and understand where it is you want to go.

I'm proud to be an independent financial advisor, and I absolutely love what I do. Nothing is more satisfying to me than working with a client toward a goal, and seeing her achieve it. I'm committed to staying abreast of changes in the financial landscape, investing in continuing education and professional development, and making sure I'm informed about the latest changes in tax laws, new financial products, and other critical issues. My clients are busy professionals. They don't have time to research the intricacies of tax laws or look up every hot stock on the market and assess whether its value is real or just the trend of the moment, and they shouldn't have to. My clients trust me to bring them the most up-to-the-minute information and help them make good financial decisions, and nothing is more important to me than honoring that trust. I'm proud of the work I do for my clients and of the relationships I build with them.

Your financial advisor should do nothing less for you. Think of financial planning as a partnership—after all, this is the person to whom you're entrusting your biggest dreams and wildest ambitions (not to mention your comfortable retirement!). Don't be snowed by a banker masquerading as a planner, or someone who's out to make a buck by selling you products you don't need and may not even understand. You want an advisor, not a salesman—someone whose first priority isn't her wallet, but your future.

In these pages, I've given you the tools you need to make the best financial advisor decision for your needs—and follow up to make sure that decision was the right one. I've poured my years of experience and passion for the field into this book, and it's been a delight for me to share what I know with you. My independent guide to financial advice is the first step toward the future you've worked so hard for and the financial security you've earned.

About the Author

MICHAEL GARRY, CFP®, JD/MBA, is a Certified Financial Planner practitioner and a member of the National Association of Personal Financial Advisors and the Financial Planning Association with over 15 years of experience. He has worked as an attorney at two successful Philadelphia law firms and a financial consultant at Merrill Lynch & Co. He oversaw the operations of Global Investment Management before forming his own company, Yardley Wealth Management, and his law firm, Yardley Estate Planning, LLC. He is regularly featured in publications such as the *Wall Street Journal, Money* magazine, *Kiplinger's*, Businessweek.com, CNNMoney.com, and Consumer Reports Money Advisor, among others.

Made in the USA
Charleston, SC
13 February 2017